TRIANGULAR PHILATELICS

A GUIDE FOR BEGINNING TO ADVANCED COLLECTORS

CHRIS GREEN

Published by

 **krause publications**

700 E. State Street • Iola, WI 54990-0001
Telephone: 715/445-2214

Please call or write for our free catalog.
Our toll-free number to place an order or obtain a free catalog is 800-258-0929 or please use our regular business telephone 715-445-2214 for editorial comment and further information.

The front cover illustrations are: A triangular issued by Monaco (top); a Nyassa Postage Due from 1924 (bottom right); a curious Cinderella item (PB140) (bottom left); and a 1935 Tannu Tuva (middle). The stamps on the back cover are Latvia's 1932 Air Post Semi-Postal and Fiume's 1920 Newspaper.

Library of Congress Catalog Number: 97-80620

ISBN: 0-87341-588-4

Printed in the United States of America

Table of Contents

Acknowledgments

The "seeds" for creating a philatelic how-to-book were planted a long time ago. My father first introduced me to stamp collecting more than 45 years ago. In addition, my parents contributed to my desire to pass on to others the outcome of my efforts. Throughout my life, I have benefited from countless how-to-books on numerous topics. Now I am able to provide a "how-to-book" so others can benefit from knowledge I have developed.

This handbook would not have been possible without the support of many people. Many collectors and dealers have provided information and items that helped in developing a more complete understanding of philatelics in general and triangulars in particular. These people are more numerous than I can specifically acknowledge here. I thank them all for their contributions.

Special acknowledgment and recognition for their significant help is appropriate for:

J. Clark Duncan, for all his contribution of information and examples from his own triangular collecting; Ginny Horn and the staff at the American Philatelic Research Library for their special assistance during the week I spent at the library (the material gathered then took over two years to process); all those at the Seattle Collector's Club who have assisted in my research efforts, particularly George, Al and Art.

A very special thank you goes to my wife, Rene, who patiently provided moral support during this book's process, from concept, through the long period of writing and to this final print.

Preface

When I started collecting triangular-shaped postage stamps, there was no list of what triangular stamps exist; there was no handbook for how to obtain triangular stamps; and there was no recognition by local stamp dealers of triangular items as the basis for a collection. I worked through every page of a complete set of worldwide catalogs to develop my initial "want" list. Over time, the initial list grew as I worked with more information sources.

I recognized how useful a specialization list and some of the "techniques" I had learned would be to other collectors. The idea of a small booklet was born. However, at this time I was also finding "strange" triangles that were not in any of the stamp catalogs. What were they? When I explored that question, it was like taking a trip to a foreign land. There was a whole other world of stamps out there–the world of the Cinderella stamp, a non-postage stamp such as a Christmas seal. Little did I realize I would eventually identify and catalog more triangular Cinderella stamps and labels than triangular postage stamps. My use of the triangular shape as the basis for a collection has led me into a breadth of Cinderella areas that would not have occurred while collecting either a country or a topical subject.

The idea for a booklet expanded to become the concept for this handbook. My objectives in writing this handbook were to:

- Provide others with guidance for having their own challenging and rewarding stamp-collecting experience.
- Help others experience more of the breadth of philately than is included in the typical stamp album; recorded in the typical catalog; and recognized by the typical stamp dealer or stamp store.
- Provide a complete and quality reference work on triangular Cinderellas.
- Provide a foundation for future philatelists and researchers in the role and impact of the triangular-shaped stamp.
- Present this new perspective on stamp collecting in a refreshing, enjoyable style.

Some of this book's content comes from my own experiences and viewpoints developed while collecting and researching triangular stamps. As such, there are subjective statements reflecting my opinion to offer insight and assist the less experienced collector to easier and more rewarding collecting.

This handbook provides a comprehensive cataloguing of triangular stamps and labels. It guides the collector through the process of finding, acquiring and identifying triangular items. The Cinderella catalog contains extensive annotation material to provide, where possible, the background and purpose of the item in addition to its physical characteristics. For those desiring to delve deeper into triangulars, there is a complete bibliography of the more than 120 references used in developing the book. Common stamp collecting terms used within the book are in an easy-to-understand glossary.

This handbook is not a price guide, but it does tell you where to get information for determining likely prices.

I hope this handbook will make stamp collecting more enjoyable for those who have not yet embarked on this adventure; and provide for the current stamp collector an intriguing new arena for collecting–triangular philatelics.

C.J.G
Seattle, Washington 1998

Triangular Treasures

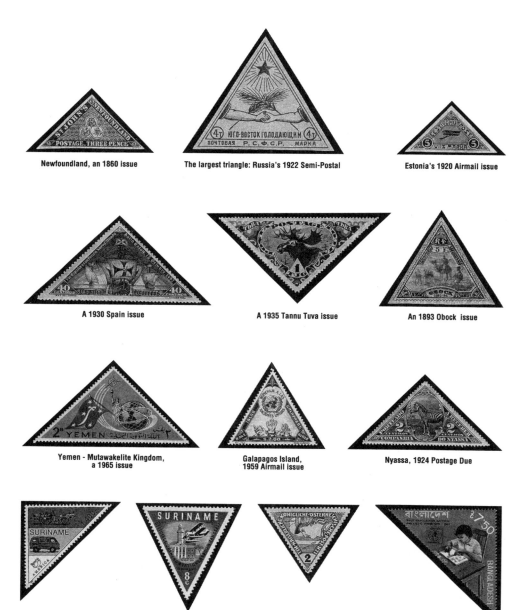

Newfoundland, an 1860 issue

The largest triangle: Russia's 1922 Semi-Postal

Estonia's 1920 Airmail issue

A 1930 Spain issue

A 1935 Tannu Tuva issue

An 1893 Obock issue

Yemen - Mutawakelite Kingdom,
a 1965 issue

Galapagos Island,
1959 Airmail issue

Nyassa, 1924 Postage Due

Suriname, 1994 issue

Suriname, 1960 issue

Austria, 1916 Special Handling

Bangladesh, 1984 issue

Chapter 1

Three Points - Three Sides

This handbook is about triangular philatelics. What is a "triangular philatelic?" Let us look at both parts of this term. "Triangular" refers to the shape of the stamp. It has three straight sides. The sides may be of different lengths, but there are only three in a triangle. "Philatelics" are stamps or stamp-like items associated with the delivery of mail and the collection of revenue (taxes and fees). Philatelics include:

- Postage stamps
- Envelopes and cards printed with the postage amount
- Stamps issued for moving mail via non-governmental companies
- Stamps used to indicate a revenue amount paid
- Labels associated with the issuance of stamps or delivery of mail, but not for postage (for example, air-mail etiquettes)
- Stamps or labels produced for use on mail, but for non-delivery purposes (for example, advertising labels)
- Items produced for collecting rather than postal use, but closely related to other philatelics (for example, stamp-exhibition labels)

Triangular stamps and labels encompass the breadth of philately. They span from the earliest of postage stamps (1853) to current day; they have been issued by countries all over the world; they have good designs and interesting subjects; and they possess a very broad range of philatelic characteristics, such as postal purpose, separation style, re-issuance and change in value.

The distinguishing feature of triangular stamps is their shape. Triangular stamps were first produced by the Cape of Good Hope. The triangular shape was used to make them readily identifiable to those handling the mail. A person can quickly detect the triangular shape as being different from the square and rectangle shapes common to most stamps. This was the reason so many of the triangle issues have been for other than normal postage.

Cape of Good Hope, 1853 issue

Australia's 1994 self-adhesive

Dominican Republic, 1960 Postal Tax

South West Africa, 1926 issue

The shape helped postal workers quickly spot the use of a special stamp. This stamp indicated a different handling than the normal mail or that a different postage rate was being used; for example: special delivery, routing to an air carrier, official business, or a special rate in effect during a specific period was being used.

Producing perforated triangulars is more difficult than producing perforated rectangular- or square-shaped stamps. Also, the postal patron finds them harder to use since the points tend to tear when being separated from a perforated sheet. This may be why some of the major countries of the world (Great Britain, Canada and France) have never issued even one triangular postage stamp, although they do have some other triangular philatelics. Also, of the countries having issued triangular stamps, 38% have issued them only once.

With the introduction of more advanced technology in mail-sorting equipment, the modern postal service has no need to use the stamp's shape as an identifier for the type of postage or delivery service. This probably means increasingly fewer new issues in the triangular shape. Triangular stamps are an integral part of postal history, even though they only make up a very small percentage of the stamps produced and used. Chapter 4, "Historical Milestones," presents, in time order, important milestones in the development, use and non-use of the triangular stamp. It adds a good historical perspective to the other information in this handbook.

Chapter 2

The Thrill of the Hunt

Collecting triangular-shaped philatelics is an interesting and rewarding activity. The number of triangular-shaped issues are a reasonably sized group–not too big and not too small. The quantity permits real progress toward putting together an interesting collection, while still having remaining challenges. Triangular stamps and labels can be bought for a few cents or up to many thousands of dollars each. Although they are available from most stamp dealers, individual stamps may be very hard to locate.

Collecting triangular stamps has little instant reward. There is a fair amount of effort involved, but this only makes the success that much sweeter.

The enjoyment comes as much from searching, exploring alternative sources, contacting new dealers, attending new shows, and certainly from meeting new people, as it does from finding the stamps themselves.

Consider the thrill of having worked to find a particular triangular stamp you have not seen before–a stamp that (maybe) the last 30 dealers you contacted did not have, but now you do!

Triangular stamps have been issued by countries throughout the world. However, they typically were not issued by the major English-speaking ones since most stamp dealers there deal with the stamps of these countries. Thus, finding triangles often requires a search for those dealers who specialize in either world-wide or the less common countries. Still, this is not a real problem since the dealer only has to have one stamp you are looking for to make it worthwhile. And the more complete your collection becomes, the more this is true.

You probably cannot walk up to a dealer, ask to see all his triangular stamps, and have him pull out an album filled with just what you want. What do you do? This handbook notes ways to succeed in your search for those next stamps.

The triangular shape is a real help to you, the collector. Like the early postal worker, you will quickly spot the triangle among all the other stamps in a dealer's albums or in display stands at stamp shows. But more on that in a later section.

1937 Australian Rocket Mail   1908 Italian Earthquake Relief Fund   1978 USA Local Post   Swiss Army Fund Raising

Triangular Philatelics takes collectors beyond postage stamps to the "world" of the Cinderella item: a stamp or label. This is a diverse and widespread area having its own histories and interesting tales associated with the items. The world of Cinderellas is composed of many different kinds of stamps and labels, with each kind having its own purpose. Triangular items exist in most of these areas. Thus, collecting triangular Cinderellas reveals the "adventures" contained within these areas. They extend over the time period of postage stamps themselves, with there being many "classic" Cinderella items.

As in the classic tale of Cinderella's glass slipper, try collecting Cinderella items and see if it is your glass slipper—see if it fits. If it does, you will have an adventure ahead of you— sometimes even like a trip through the looking glass (but that is another tale). These stamps have mystery, romance and adventure. Consider the terms used to describe several of the Cinderella areas: "bogus," "phantoms," "revenues," "propaganda labels," "pigeon post," "rocket mail," and "postal strike." These are indicative of a lesser-charted area of stamp collecting waiting for you to discover.

A Toy Stamp

1897 Belgium Exhibition Label

Belgium Advertising Label

There has not been a published contemporary guide or list of triangular stamps before this handbook. Considerable research has been done to assemble the information provided herein, and is still continuing. Rather than wait until I was done with tracking down all the appropriate entries for a handbook such as this, I am making my findings available now. I hope others will explore *Triangular Philatelics*, decide to collect triangulars and gain the same kind of enjoyment and satisfaction as I have.

The small number of new triangulars being issued is a plus for collecting triangles. When there is a small number of items issued each year, the collector does not have to spend large amounts to keep up with the new issues. This is in marked contrast to what has been happening with the USA's postal service. Here, the number of new issues, and the total cost per year, has been growing rapidly.

Before my concentration on triangulars, I collected both USA and Great Britain, but found it was becoming very expensive for little fun and enjoyment. I realized I like hunting stamps as much, if not more, than owning them. Triangular philatelics provides a breadth and variety to collecting, a limited enough set of items so as to be accomplishable, challenges in locating the harder-to-find stamps, and lots of rewards along the way as stamps are discovered and acquired.

Chapter 3

Triangular Trivia

This is a presentation of miscellaneous facts and trivia about triangular postage stamps issued from 1853 through 1996. These facts and figures relate to all issued items excluding proofs, essays, errors, reprints, and souvenir sheets.

Reviewing statistics about the issuance of triangulars helps to understand the role they have played in the history of philately.

In this handbook, the following definitions apply:

- An **item** is a stamp, label or seal.
- Items are issued in groups called **sets**, even when there is only one item in the set. An issue is usually all the items originated on a particular date.
- An **issue** is considered to have been created when there is some aspect to a set of stamps that differs from previous issues. This might be the color, design and denomination; or it might be overprinting or surcharging. These all create a new issue.

When there is a philatelic term in this handbook you are not familiar with, check Chapter 13, "Philatelic Terminology." For these statistics, both halves of a perforated bisect are included as one item. Also, when a set was issued with different separations (perforate, imperforate or roulette) it is counted as only one issue. Overprints and surcharges do create new issues since there was a postal need for the particular "added printing," done to eliminate designing and producing new stamps. The number of stamps does count the difference in separations.

Trivia regarding all of the triangular postage stamps

- There have been 331 issues of triangles.
- These issues produced a total of 1,655 different stamps.
- These issues were done by 105 different countries. Note: When a country became a different country during this period, it is counted as two separate countries.

1956 Monaco   1894 Liberia   1865 Colombia   1964 Sharjah

Issuance of triangulars

- Triangles have been issued for 15 different types of postal services and delivery options.
- The largest number of triangular items issued in a single set are the 22 items on transportation issued by Monaco for regular mail use in 1956.
- Liberia has created the largest number of triangular issues, 25, from 1894 to 1953.

- Colombia has issued triangulars over the longest time period, 123 years, from 1865 through 1987; but from 1870 through 1968, it issued no triangulars.
- Surinam has issued the largest number of triangular items, 117.
- Sharjah issued the largest number of triangular items in the shortest time period: 104 items from 1964-66. Weren't they busy! (See the notes regarding "Black Blots" in Chapter 5).
- The largest number of triangular items issued within a single year is 52, issued by Jordan in 1964. (Again, see the notes regarding "Black Blots.")
- There are 44 countries that have had only one issuance of triangulars.
- The 1960s had the largest number of items issued, 591. These were issued by 45 different countries, which is also the largest number of countries to issue within any decade.

Particular item trivia

- The first triangular postage stamp was issued in 1853 by the Cape of Good Hope.
- The first perforated triangulars were issued by Ecuador in 1908.
- The latest triangular issued: Since they are still being issued by several countries each year, you will have to determine the latest one yourself.
- The largest triangle issued is Russia's 1922 semi-postal issue.
- The smallest triangle is Colombia's 1869 regular mail issue.
- The first triangle having its apex at the bottom of the design was Austria's special-handling stamps of 1916.
- The only scalene triangle ever issued is Colombia's 1869 regular mail issue.

First perforated triangle: 1908 Ecuador

The smallest triangle: 1869 Colombia

Issue having most variations: 1909 Liberia

- The first equilateral triangle (its three sides are all the same length) is Colombia's 1865 issue.
- The single triangular design with the most variants is the one Liberia used from 1909 through 1918. This has a reclining lady with a ship's anchor. There are 14 variations created by changes in color, separations and overprints, or surcharges.
- The first self-adhesive triangle is Australia's 1994 set.

Recent issues — 1997

Marshall Islands

New Zealand

United States of America

For more statistical information on triangulars, see the Appendix, which has tables of additional data.

Chapter 4

Historical Milestones

Triangular postage stamps have been used for the past 144 years. A review of key triangular issues gives us an indication of the role they have played throughout postal history. It reveals their shape has been both the reason for their use and the reason they have not had wider usage. This chapter provides a chronological overview of important happenings with triangular-shaped postage and is a condensation of my article, "The History of the Triangular Postage Stamp," published by Linn's Stamp News on Feb. 17, 1997.

The first triangular issue was the 1853 Cape of Good Hope stamp, whose three-sided shape had a definite postal function. The triangle was designed to distinguish letters originating in the colony itself from those coming in from mail overseas. The story goes that this was intended to help semi-literate native clerks sort the mail correctly. Over the next 10 years, Cape of Good Hope produced 12 more triangular stamps (see illustration in Chapter 1).

The second country to issue a triangular stamp was Newfoundland, another British colony. From 1857 to 1860, its postal service printed a set of nine stamps ranging in value from 1 penny to 1 shilling. Of these, the 3d denomination was a green, triangular design showing the rose, thistle, and shamrock, the heraldic flowers of the United Kingdom. Newfoundland dropped the 3d value when its second set was produced in 1861, and never used the triangular shape again. (See the *Triangular Treasures* illustration page).

These first two triangular issues were imperforate and had to be cut apart with scissors, which may have been inconvenient for post-office clerks and patrons.

Imperforate triangles are almost as easy to produce as rectangular stamps. Both of these early stamps are right-angle triangles, with one angle of 90 degrees and two 45-degree angles. This made sheets easy to produce, since two right-angle stamps placed hypotenuse-to-hypotenuse form a square. This format has been used in 75 percent of all triangular issues.

In 1865, Colombia produced a different type of stamp, an equilateral triangle, in which all three sides are the same length and the angles are all 60 degrees (see illustration in Chapter 3). This requires a different, and rather more complicated, arrangement of the stamps on a sheet for printing and eventual separation. About 17 percent of all triangular issues have been in this equilateral format.

In 1869, Colombia produced a triangular stamp unique in two respects: It is the smallest triangular postage stamp and the only one ever issued as a scalene triangle, which has three different length sides and three different angles (see illustration in Chapter 3).

Obock, a port city in what is now Djibouti, produced triangular stamps in 1892 and 1894. Although Obock's Camel and Rider issues are imperforate, they have printing around the border of the design that simulates perforations. At that time, perforation machines could not yet follow the patterns needed to perforate triangular stamps (*Triangular Treasures*).

Some stamps featured rouletting, a series of slits cut between stamps as a way to separate them. Liberia first employed this method on a 5-cent triangular stamp in 1894, and went on to roulette several of its triangular stamps until 1919.

When Ecuador produced the first perforated triangular stamps in 1908 (see illustration in Chapter 3) - the five middle values in a seven-stamp set showing men who had a role in creating the rail line from Guayaquil to Quito - perforated rectangular stamps had been in use for 53 years. Ecuador's issue was followed by several perforated Liberian triangular issues during 1909-15.

In 1911, a perforated triangular stamp was created, not by design, but as a result of Paraguay running short of its 20-centavo regular postage stamps. It had a surplus of the 75-centavo stamp, issued in the previous year. These stamps perforated diagonally, that is they bisected the 75-c rectangular to create two triangular stamps sold and used as 20-c stamps.

After 1915, as suitable machinery became available, most countries perforated their triangular stamps, which made them much easier for postal patrons to separate and use.

The triangular stamp's distinctive appearance is part of the reason so many of them were issued for services and postal duties different from those of ordinary postage stamps. In a busy sorting room, postal workers could quickly spot the unusual shape and sort out any mail bearing such postage, which indicated different handling was required.

In 1916, Austria issued two triangular printed-matter special handling stamps. These were the first designed to have their apex at the bottom, pointing downward. An imperforate copy of the striking 2-heller Mercury stamps is illustrated in *Triangular Treasures*.

Fiume used triangular stamps to mail newspapers in 1919 to 1920. The designs of these three items, which also have their apex at the bottom, make excellent use of the three-sided shape.

Estonia, the first country with a triangular airmail stamp, is also the only one to use the shape for all of its airmail issues—18 stamps released from 1920 to 1925. This is a good example of using a stamp's shape to help identify the class of mail service. The first, a 5-mark stamp, is shown in *Triangular Treasures*. The first 13 stamps were imperforate, but Estonia perforated the final five.

The largest triangular stamp ever produced is the Soviet Union's 1922 imperforate 4,000-ruble semi-postal. With a base measuring 2 1/2 inches from tip to tip, it is six and a half times the size of the smallest three-sided stamp (*Triangular Treasures*).

Collecting postage due was a good opportunity for a distinctively shaped stamp to help the delivery person recognize additional payment was required upon delivery. The first triangular postage-due stamps were created in 1924 by Nyassa, now part of Mozambique. A 10-c stamp from this 73-year-old set, one of three showing the flagship San Gabriel of Vasco da Gama, has a strong resemblance to the 1997 United States 32-cent triangular Ship.

In 1928, Mozambique issued the first triangular postal tax stamps. This set was issued as a way to raise money for the Cross of the Orient Society, a Red Cross agency. It had to be used for all mail on certain days of the year. Mozambique had used rectangular shaped stamps for this postal tax for two years before it switched to the triangular shape—probably because it was easier to recognize on those days when it was required postage (see illustration in Chapter 5).

In 1937, Czechoslovakia issued two 50-haler triangular personal-delivery stamps—one in blue, the other red (see illustration in Chapter 5). Payment of the extra fee represented by these stamps assured personal delivery directly to the addressee and no one else. But why two 50-h triangular stamps? Senders who wanted personal delivery bought red stamps. However, when addressees wanted all their mail delivered personally, they bought blue stamps the post office affixed to their letters before delivery.

The triangular shape was first used on postal stationery—envelopes or postal cards pre-printed with the postage amount—by the United States with a 1956 postcard issued in conjunction with FIPEX, the Fifth International Philatelic Exhibition in New York.

In the 1960s, many countries issued triangular stamps primarily for sale to collectors to create additional postal revenue. The subjects on many of these stamps often had no relation to the nations that issued them. Those who made and marketed much of this material merely saw the three-sided shape as something different, another gimmick to attract stamp collectors, even as Cape of Good Hope triangles had been the sensation of stamp collecting when they first became available in Europe more than a century before.

The shape of the triangular stamp is its weakness, even as its distinctive appearance is its strength. Due to the difficulty in printing and separating these stamps, 38 percent of the countries which have issued triangular stamps have done so only once.

In 1994, the first self-adhesive triangular stamps—stylized copper-foil kangaroos with backgrounds in eight different colors, produced in se-tenant booklets of 20—were issued by Australia (see illustration in Chapter 1). Like most self-adhesives, these stamps are die cut, a format in which the triangle is no harder to produce than any other shape. In fact, the pointed triangular corners make these self-adhesive stamps easier to lift off the backing sheet than many rectangular ones.

Thus, Australia's self-adhesive triangle avoids the production and separation drawbacks of conventional triangular stamps. With the growing demand for self-adhesive stamps, we just might see triangles being used more and more frequently.

Chapter 5

Setting Your Sights

This chapter provides a comprehensive look at the characteristics of the triangular shape; the kinds of philatelic items where triangulars have been used; and your role in defining your collection. The information here is a foundation for building your triangular collection. It also provides terminology specific to the triangulars.

PHYSICAL PROPERTIES OF TRIANGULARS

Let us examine the physical properties of triangulars and the terms used in describing them.

Review of an old high school geometry book indicates there are six types of triangular shapes:

Right angle: In this triangle, one of the angles is a right angle of 90 degrees.

Isosceles: This triangle has two sides of equal length and two angles of the same degrees.

Equilateral: In this triangle, the sides are the same length and the angles are each 60 degrees.

Obtuse: One of the angles in this triangle is greater than 90 degrees.

Acute: All of the angles are less than 90 degrees.

Scalene: All the sides are different lengths and the angles are different degrees.

| A right angle isosceles, Nicaragua's 1947 Official Air Post | An obtuse, from Lithuania in 1991 | An acute, a Netherland Antilles 1955 issue | An equilateral, Uruguay's 1929 Parcel Post |

A triangular stamp has only three sides and three points. It will also have a design on it, and usually an orientation for viewing the design–that is, a definite top and bottom to the design. (I say usually because there are a few triangulars for which there is no top or bottom, but instead three equal orientations.) The **base** of the triangle is the horizontal side, when the stamp is viewed from the intended orientation. The base may be the longest side, but it can be any side. The base may or may not be on the bottom of the design. The **apex** is the point of the triangle opposite the base and may be above or below it.

This all provides for a broad range of possible arrangements of the design relative to the shape and intended orientation of the stamp. See examples on the Triangular Treasures page.

The **design** of the stamp is what is printed on the paper, excluding the denomination and any overprinting applied after the initial stamp production. (The **denomination** of the stamp is the printed price–the price paid for the stamp for its use as postage). The design

Triangular Components

This page illustrates the parts of a triangular stamp.

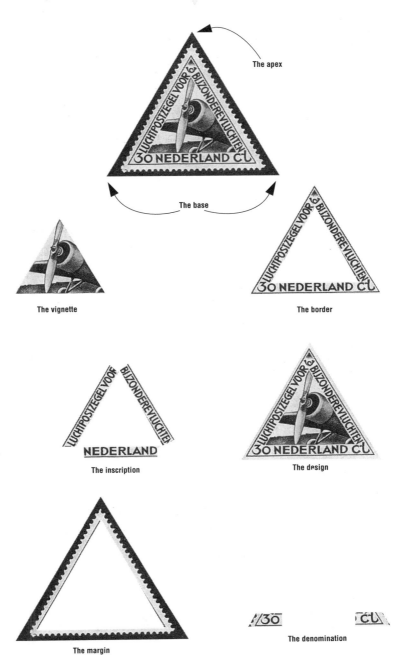

The apex

The base

The vignette

The border

The inscription

The design

The margin

The denomination

does not include the colors used in the printing. This means a set of stamps may have only one design, while the items have different colors and denominations.

The **border** of the stamp, if there is one, is a band around the outer edge of the design, usually on all three sides. It often contains words and values stating the country, the reason for issuance or the denomination of the stamp.

The **vignette** is the area within the borders when there are borders, otherwise it is the entire design of the stamp.

KINDS OF TRIANGULAR ITEMS

The triangular items covered in this handbook are categorized into seven groups. The first five groupings are items issued by a governmental postal authority to pay for postal services, or they are an item closely allied to those stamps. The sixth and seventh groups contain all the non-postal items.

Postage stamps

These are the various postal services and delivery options for which countries have issued postage stamps in a triangular shape:

Air post: Created for use on items for transport by a carrier flying the mail as a major part of its delivery.

Air post official: Stamps used for governmental mail using air delivery.

Air post semi-postal: These stamps had part of their cost designated for some non-postal purpose, often a welfare cause. With these items, the delivery was by an air carrier.

Newspaper: These were created specifically for the shipment of newspapers.

Netherlands' 1933 Air Post   Iceland's 1930 Air Post Official   Latvia's 1932 Air Post Semi-Postal   Fiume's 1920 Newspaper

Official: These stamps were created for general governmental mail and sometimes created by overprinting of regular stamps.

Parcel post: These stamps were used for a different service and rate for mailing parcels.

Personal delivery: These stamps were used to ensure the mail was delivered only to the addressee.

Postage due: Special stamps used by the postal authorities to indicate an amount owed by the recipient, due to insufficient postage having been originally applied.

Postal tax: These were not valid for postage, but used to raise money for a specified purpose and were obligatory during certain time periods or with certain kinds of mail.

Guatemala's 1929 Official issue   Czechoslovakia's 1937 Personal Delivery   Bolivia's 1931 Postage Due   Mozambique's 1928 Postal Tax

Postal tax semi-postal: A semi-postal is a stamp that has a part of its cost for other purposes; a postal tax is a fee for other than postage.

Registered: These stamps are for the service whereby the postal system keeps specific records on the handling of individual pieces of mail.

Regular mail: Stamps used for general and non-specific postal purposes. They indicate the amount paid, which can apply to all types of postal services.

Semi-postal: These stamps had part of their cost designated for a non-postal purpose, often a charitable cause. Usually the stamp cost is printed in two parts–one indicating the postal amount, the other indicating the amount for charity. Thus, "25c + 5c" overprinted on a stamp indicates 25c for the postal purpose and 5c for the charitable contribution.

Special delivery: The sender pays an extra fee to have the item delivered immediately upon arrival at the destination post office. These stamps are for this extra cost.

Special handling: These stamps were used on parcels to give them the same service as first-class items.

1921 Liberian Registered mail

1987 Colombia Special Delivery

1947 Brazil Postal Tax Semi-Postal

1918 Semi-Postal from Liberia

Postal stationery

Postal stationery are those postcards, envelopes and air letters issued by postal services with a pre-printed stamp.

Souvenir sheets

Souvenir sheets are issued by postal services primarily for stamp collectors. They usually promote or commemorate some particular event and often contain more than one stamp, plus other commemorative information around the stamps. The stamp(s) may be perforate, imperforate or roulette in the sheet. A common contemporary trend is for the souvenir sheet to depict an entire scene in often colorful and attractive art, with the stamp being a small piece out of the actual scene. Although not intended for postal purposes, they typically can be used for postage and thus sometimes are found in used condition.

Some countries issue them primarily as a way to raise additional money. Often they have a much higher price than the normal stamps, and may not commemorate anything of significance for the issuing country.

Bisects

Bisects are partial stamps used for postage. Typically it is half a stamp, hence the term (from bisected). Some stamps have even been cut into thirds or fourths. When a stamp is made into a two-part bisect, it can have been a vertical splitting, a horizontal splitting or a

Triangular Souvenir Sheets

These are items issued by postal services primarily for stamp collectors. They usually promote or commemorate some particular event. They often contain more than one stamp plus other commemorative information around the stamps. Below are some examples of the diversity found in triangular souvenir sheets.

St. Vincent issued in 1996

Hungary issued in 1958

Spain's 1992 Semi-Postal

Panama issued in 1964

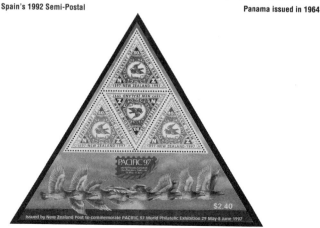

New Zealand issued in 1997

diagonal splitting from one corner to the opposite corner. The diagonally split stamps are triangular and part of triangular philatelics.

Typically, bisects were created by the postal service when it ran out of lower-value stamps, used for regular local postings, and it still had a supply of higher-denomination stamps used for parcels or non-local mailings. This often happened in rural areas, where the re-supply of stamps did not occur frequently. The post office would cut the higher-value stamps and affix them. People then realized they also could cut the stamps, but sometimes they recycled used stamps by cutting away the half that had a cancellation on it. So, just prior to 1900, bisects generally stopped being accepted as valid stamps in most countries.

Mozambique 1961 Postal Stationery | 1935 Guatemala bisect | 1951 Guatemala Airmail bisect | 1911 Paraguay bisect

There are situations where a government had a large oversupply of high-denomination items and a shortage of lower denominations. It re-perforated the sheets of stamps to create bisects prior to distribution to its post offices. Some of these were re-perforated on the diagonal, thus creating a triangular item.

For most bisects to be recognized by philatelists, it must be really clear they are genuine. It is preferred to have them on a cover. When they were created by perforation or there was overprinting involved in their creation, then a loose stamp can be acceptable. Otherwise, a loose stamp could be a regular stamp someone cut in half after it was used as a whole stamp, thus it would not be a postally valid bisect.

This edition of *Triangular Philatelics* only includes diagonally perforated bisects created by postal authorities. Diagonal bisects created by cutting the stamp will be covered in a future edition.

Triangular stamps-on-stamps

Stamps-on-stamps is a topical category. Stamps in this category depict other stamps in their design. Triangular stamps-on-stamps are those whose design illustrate triangular-shaped stamps. The triangular stamp depicted has been important enough to the postal history of a country that it has included it as a subject for a stamp. These stamps are not triangular shaped.

1990 Anguilla | 1975 Costa Rica Airmail | 1953 South Africa | 1968 Paraguay

This category is included in *Triangular Philatelics* because these stamps depict recognition by postal authorities of the philatelic importance of the (triangular) stamps illustrated.

Some of the triangular stamps appearing on other stamps include the Cape of Good Hope, diagonal bisects, and even a Cinderella local post.

Revenues

Revenues are stamps used to indicate a duty or tax paid to the issuing authority in the amount of the stamp and for the purpose stated on the stamp. These are also called fiscals.

Cinderellas

Cinderellas are all other postally related items not covered in the above classifications. Postally related means the items were intended for use on envelopes or packages mailed via a postal authority. A common example of this type of item is the Christmas seal—it is intended for people to use on letters, but not for actual postal purposes. An example of what is not included is an airline baggage label, intended for use on luggage.

Sometimes it can be unclear whether a particular item is a Cinderella. Some catalogs will list particular items, while other catalogers do not. One cataloger may have evaluated an item as not having been issued for valid postal purposes, thus it is a Cinderella. The same item evaluated by another cataloger as having been issued for postal purposes is thus listed as a postage stamp. One of the best known examples of this is the Tanna Tuva issues after 1933. As of its 1997 catalog, Scott Publishing does not list these items. However, Michel, the major German cataloging company, does catalog them as postage stamps.

Some of the Cinderella classifications relate directly to postal purposes. These include ettiquettes, railway stamps, postal strike stamps, local posts, and other types of airmail stamps. The items were not from a governmental postal authority for payment of postage. For an interesting, well-written overview of Cinderellas, see *Mackay's Stamp Collecting*.

The number of Cinderella items for all kinds and categories is huge. There are so many items, in fact, one can not reasonably expect to have a complete general collection—that would be like having a complete general collection of world-wide postage stamps, something very few people can do. Thus, a focus on some specific aspect of Cinderellas gives a more limited set of items. Collecting based on the triangular shape provides one such focus.

Collecting Cinderellas is more challenging than collecting postage stamps because there are far fewer sources available for finding the items. The items occur infrequently with most dealers and take considerable work to locate. The hunt for certain items can take months or even years, but then the reward is more gratifying after succeeding.

Various authors, Cinderella clubs and Cinderella auctions have used different classification schema. *Triangular Philatelics* classifies Cinderellas with a composite schema derived from these other sources. The ordering of the classifications is alphabetical and does not signify the relative importance of the classification.

Labels and seals

Adhesive labels and seals exist for many purposes, but most were used on letters in addition to the postage stamps. The sender used them to let others know of an event, business or charity they support.

The sub-classifications of labels and seals are:

- Charity fund-raising
- Etiquettes—airmail
- Etiquettes—COD
- Letter seals
- Publicity—advertisements
- Publicity—commemorative

- Publicity–propaganda
- World wars–Delandre
- World wars–other military
- World wars–patriotic
- World wars–Swiss army

Note: The sub-classifications of labels and seals do not include issues specifically related to stamp collecting. Those are in a separate classification called Philatelica.

Locals

Locals are stamps issued for use within a small area, a city, town or over a limited route. They have been issued by governmental agencies, municipalities and private concerns. The routes have usually filled a void left by the governmental services in the surrounding areas. Mail deliveries from islands without regular mail coverage have often used local services to get the mail to a location served by the country's normal mail channels.

On the rare occasions when a governmental postal service goes on strike, there are businessmen ready to establish alternative delivery services. These services invariably use stamps to pre-pay their deliveries just as the post office does.

Railway lines sometimes expedited the delivery of a letter or parcel. To pay for this service, they issued railway stamps. Typically, both the railway and normal postage were used–the item would be "mailed" at the local train station, taken by rail to the destination city, and then placed in the regular postal system to complete the delivery.

The sub-classifications include the above mentioned local posting:

- Modern
- Pre-1950
- Postal strike
- Railway

Other airmail

Other airmail are items used to pay postage for carrying a correspondence via some way through the air. Private organizations or companies operated these services, although they may have had the blessing of the local postal authorities.

In the early 1930s, many countries experimented with using rockets for delivering mail. Promoters sold postage stamps to raise money and help finance the experiments. Letters carried in the rockets used the stamps to pay for their mailing.

The sub-classifications of other airmail include:

- Essay and semi-official
- Pigeon post
- Rocket mail

Phantoms and bogus

Phantoms and bogus stamps are some of the most interesting Cinderellas, at least as far as having colorful backgrounds. A phantom is for a country or entity that has never existed, an imaginary country, or an imaginary local post. A bogus is a stamp for a country or entity that has existed, but never issued the particular item. It is not a copy of something else issued; rather, it is something that conceivably could have been legitimately issued. I strongly recommend searching out some reference articles for the stamps in this classification. A good general, although old, reference for this area is *Phantom Philately* REF#3610.

Philatelica

This is a group of labels and seals specifically related to stamp collecting. Not surprisingly, organizations or businesses whose major activity related to stamp collecting have produced their own issues. They were issued as dealer's advertising, commemorative items for historically important philatelic events and souvenirs for philatelic exhibitions.

The sub-classifications are:

- Advertising
- Commemorative
- Exhibitions
- Organizations

Miscellaneous

This is the "catch-all" classification–a place for the really different or unclassifiable material. Explore the section for this classification in the Cinderella listing to find out more about this group.

The sub-classifications are:

- Artistamps
- Postal savings stamps
- Postal stationery
- Se-tenant tabs
- Toy stamps
- Triangular stamps-on-stamps
- Not classified

DEFINING YOUR COLLECTION

Defining what your collection will contain is determined by you. It is not made by the spaces in a stamp album. It is not made by the entries in a catalog. It is not made by the postal services that continue to issue large numbers of new issues. *You* make the determination.

When arriving at that definition you will consider:

- Collecting only mint, only used or both?
- Collecting only postage stamps, only Cinderellas or both?
- Collecting for all time periods, or stopping at a certain year or starting at a certain year?
- Collecting only stamps, only covers or both?
- Collecting a particular country, or group of countries or topic, or , as in the case of triangulars, a particular shape?
- Collecting a particular type of stamp; for example, only airmail stamps?

This gives you an idea of some of the aspects of a collection you will either explicitly decide on, or which will arise as you find and purchase items.

To assist you in developing an initial definition of what you might want to collect, study this handbook, particularly the illustrations. Look at items in a stamp catalog. Talk to other collectors about what they collect and why. Recognize what interests you and start your collecting. Do it for awhile to see how it fits with your own nature, then re-examine your "collection definition" to see if it really fits or if you need to modify it.

Of course, you can just go and buy stamps without a really clear idea of what your collecting boundaries are. Some collectors buy only items they really like–and that is the only

Triangular Covers

A "cover" is a complete envelope. It contains the stamps, the cancellations, the address, maybe a return address, and possibly other interesting markings or taggings that were applied as it went through the delivery process. Illustrated here are three types of covers.

Normal postal use

Covers in this group are the result of something being sent using some type of mail service. They have no aspects that were created for stamp-collecting reasons. They may have many different features. However, all the features were necessary for getting the item from the sender to the recipient at the time and places involved, via the sender's desired delivery service, and conforming to postal regulations.

This example is of a very simple usage with few features. Although these Nicaragua triangulars were issued in August 1947, these were not used until June 11, 1949. However, the post office had not issued any other airmail stamps during the intervening period. These two, plus another stamp, were used to have the required total of 55 centavos for an international air letter.

First day cover

These are (usually special) envelopes mailed on the date when its stamps were first available. Stamp catalogs give the date of a stamp's first issue.

This example has many features. It was mailed from Dunedin, New Zealand, on Oct. 1, 1943, using one each of the two semi-postal stamps issued that day. This semi-postal issue had an amount of each stamp's price that went to support children's health camps (1/2d was added to the 1d stamp, and 1d was added to the 2d stamp). This cover was addressed to a USA destination.

World War II postal regulations were in effect. The letter was examined for inappropriate content, and then resealed by application of a label inscribed, "OPENED BY EXAMINER D.D.A. / 13." This label is primarily on the cover's backside. The front-right edge of the envelope shows part of the label with the inscription, "P.C.--90."

When it arrived in Pendleton, Oregon, on Oct. 31, it could not be delivered to the designated recipient. The Pendleton post office handstamped it three times with, "Do not use this envelope again   RETURNED TO SENDER   UNCLAIMED From Pendleton, Oregon." It has a further date stamp of Nov. 2, which is probably when it was sent back to New Zealand. The date stampings are on the back of the cover.

Philatelic cover

This type of cover was specifically created for a stamp-collecting purpose. The most common of these is when all the stamps in an issue were used on an envelope, even though not necessary to meet the required postal rate.

This example from Haiti uses all six of the triangulars issued in May 1962. Although the front is canceled with May 30, 1962, the first day of issue, on the back is a cancellation for when it really was sent, June 2. This item was prepared and sent only to create the cover. There was only a blank piece of heavy paper inside the envelope. It arrived in Illinois on June 4, according to the receipt cancellation on the back.

criteria for their collection. They may not be able to tell before seeing an item whether they want it, but their style of collecting does not diminish their rewards.

For a particular "collection" to be worthwhile, it needs two characteristics: It needs to be obtainable and require some effort. When it is too easy, the reward is not adequate. The goal of having a very complete collection of triangular philatelics meets both of these criteria.

The nice thing about defining your collection is you can change your definition whenever you choose. Keep in mind it is *your* collection and there are no wrong or right definitions as to what you include. So long as your collection provides *you* enjoyment, it is the right one for you.

TO INCLUDE OR NOT INCLUDE

The issue of a "legitimate" stamp versus an "illegitimate" one and their place in your collection is a topic that can cause considerable consternation. The reason for the original issuance of the item is the clearest delineator between legitimate and illegitimate. The purpose for a legitimate stamp was other than just ending up in a stamp collector's album. A stamp, either postal or Cinderella, is illegitimate when its reason for being was for sale to stamp collectors.

Unfortunately, it is sometimes hard to determine the real reason behind the creation of some items. Consider the case of many souvenir sheets–what purpose did they serve other than to raise money for the postal service that issued them? Consider issues from countries that printed 20 to 50 times the number of stamps needed for postal use by the people in the country. These items are often available in both mint and CTO form. The CTOs were because the postal service wanted to create the impression of their legitimacy and there would have been too few postally used items to achieve that "respectability."

In 1962, many items with little postal validity were being created expressly for sale to collectors. The volume of these items became so large the American Philatelic Society published monthly, in the *American Philatelist,* a list of countries and issues highly suspected of being illegitimate. These stamps of dubious purpose received a "Black Blot" (REF#7030).

In May of 1962, the APS started to raise the awareness of the prevalency of non-postal issues by certain countries. It established five criteria for determining the non-postal nature of an issue:

- A limited printing or limited time on sale.
- An excessive number of items in the issue from either many designs or from denominations beyond postal needs.
- Unwarranted high-value denominations.
- No direct relationship to the issuing country–these are often with popular topics included in the designs.
- Oddities intentionally included with the issue; for example, issuing a second overprinting in a different color and with a different direction of printing.

  They detected such practices as:
- Issuing 5.5 million perforated copies of a stamp, but only 10,000 copies of the same stamp in imperf form.
- Countries shipping 90% of an issue for sale in places outside the country.
- Countries issuing airmail stamps, when the country did not even have any airports.
- Long sets of stamps not being used or needed in the issuing country for mailings.
- Creation of extensive oddity items, including limited issue of imperf stamps, souvenir sheets not useable for mailing and overprinting in different colors.

In 1965, the FIP (Federation Internationale de Philatelie) joined the campaign. It went so far as to place a ban on particular items and particular countries' stamps appearing in FIP

Triangular Pairs

There are several different arrangements of two or more triangulars that can arise from the way they were printed on the full sheet. Four of these are illustrated and explained below.

Imperf pair

When the separator between two stamps is imperforate, that is no holes or slits, only a pair of the stamps can really show the stamps were originally produced imperf. When a stamp comes in both perf and imperf varieties, it is possible for someone to have trimmed away the perf holes of a perf stamp to create a more valuable imperf. This example is from Liberia's 1936 Airmail set.

Se-tenant pair

This pair is two stamps of different designs produced next to each other. When a set of stamps contains multiple designs, the designs could have been produced one per sheet of stamps. Or they could have been produced with the different designs occurring on the same sheet. The latter situation is a se-tenant sheet. This example is two of eight from Nevis' only triangular set.

Tete-beche pair

This pair is two adjacent stamps where the design in one is upside down relative to the other. Once separated, one cannot tell the stamps were printed tete-beche. Neither stamp has any printing that is upside down on the single stamp. Obviously, the collector needs to obtain an unseparated pair to portray this philatelic condition. This term comes from the French for "head the wrong way." This example is from a 1965 Sharjah issue.

'Super' triangle

This refers to a group of unseparated stamps where the shape of the set of stamps is itself a triangle. Whether this can occur for an item depends on the arrangement of the triangles on the original sheet being manufactured. It takes a minimum of four stamps to make a super-triangle; that is, one on the top, one in the center, one on the right side and one on the left side. This example is from the 1975 St. Vincent triangular issue.

exhibitions. The federation put out an eight-point list of criteria for evaluating Undesirable Issues (REF#7030Jan.1965/275).

In 1968, Stanley Gibbons Catalogues stopped listing these Undesirables along with the country, and instead put them in a special Appendix. Countries issuing triangles that were Black-Blotted during the 1960s include: Afghanistan, Albania, Bhutan, Burundi, Cook Islands, East Germany, Ecuador, Fujeria, Guinea, Haiti, Hungary, Jordan, Khor Fakkan, Lybia, Maldive Islands, Nigeria, Panama, Qatar, Qu'aiti State in Hadhramaut, Romania, Sharjah, and Yemen. For most of these countries, it was only part of their issues that were undesirable; for others, it was many of their issues. Issuing unnecessary imperfs and souvenir sheets not for postal use were the main offenses.

The American Philatelic Society issued its Black-Blot warnings until 1981, when it seemed to have stopped without any explanation as to why it was abandoning its 19-year effort.

Should you collect possibly illegitimate issues? In deliberating "illegitimates," consider the following aspects:

- The stamps do exist.
- They were created for a distinct purpose, even when that purpose was to transfer money from stamp collectors to dealers or to the treasury of particular countries.
- These items tend to still be at a very (artificially) high price.
- Although they may not meet criteria for being postally valid, they certainly are valid as Cinderella items.

The answer to "collect or not?" is your choice. Just like the rest of your collection, *you* are the one who sets the boundaries.

Chapter 6

Getting Equipped

There are a few philatelic supplies that will aid your collecting. Some are to help you in working with the stamps, and some are for the preservation of the stamps themselves.

Tools

You should never handle stamps with your fingers. Use stamp tongs. This tweezer-like tool will, after some practice, permit you to pick up, move and place your stamps where you want without running the risk of soiling them. Your fingers can leave an acid on the stamp which can disturb the gum on mint items. Over a long period, this can be detrimental to the condition of the item.

One of the necessary tools to have for working with variations of a stamp is the "perforation gauge." This device helps determine the number of perforation holes in 2 centimeters. This is the worldwide standard for the specification of a perforation size. The perforations are "measured" with the perf gauge. It is the same as using a ruler, except instead of determining length, it counts the "holes."

A magnifying glass is a useful tool for determining variations of a stamp. Often the variations in a stamp's design occur from one issuance to another, particularly when several years may have elapsed between issues. Often these variations are fairly subtle and require a better look at the stamp through a magnifying glass.

Stamp storage and display

Traditionally, stamp collections are stored in stamp albums. However, several alternative storage aids can be more suitable for collecting triangulars. Unlike collecting a specific country's stamps, where ready-made stamp albums exist with places to mount each stamp, there is no album specifically for triangular-shaped stamps.

There are four alternatives for organizing and storing your stamps. You can use albums, stock books, plastic pages or glassine envelopes, or a combination of these to meet your particular needs.

Whatever you use for storing your stamps, it needs to protect the stamps and be non-harmful to them. The storage materials must be chemically neutral. Mounting stamps on regular paper stock is not adequate–acid-free paper must be used, otherwise the residual chemicals in the paper are likely to harm your philatelic gems.

Consider using a blank album or album pages available from philatelic suppliers to create an album for triangulars. These pages are made of the right kind of paper. When using an album, you also have to choose if, when or how you will use stamp hinges. Stamp hinges are little, pre-folded bits of thin, gummed paper you use to stick the stamp to the album. The concern is the impact on the stamp. When a stamp is mint, then the act of hinging *will* disturb the stamp's gum no matter how careful you are. This lessens the value of the stamp–the more valuable the stamp, the greater the decrease in value. For your better items, you can use stamp mounts. These are usually clear plastic with a black backing paper made so the stamp slips inside. The mount is the part stuck to the album page, not the stamp.

Stock books, available from philatelic suppliers, have long pockets to hold the stamps. Usually only half the stamp is in the pocket. Pockets may be clear or not. The stamps are not stuck down, so there is no lessening of the stamps' quality, but they also are partly unprotected.

Pages made of clear plastic on top of a black card stock are available and provide a very attractive way for storing your stamps. It permits seeing each individual item and allows moving the items around to get a better organization as your collection grows. These pages also come in many forms to accommodate different size items–from conventional stamp sizes, up to complete envelopes, long strips or even complete pages. They are typically 8 1/2-inch by 11-inch pages ready for insertion into a three- or four-ring binder. Thus, one can easily insert additional pages to accommodate more items. There are many brands available that can be found at your local stamp dealer or obtained via mail order from many firms that advertise in philatelic publications.

With the plastic sheet pages, there are no mounting hinges; thus, the condition of your stamps remains without the lessening that occurs with the use of hinges, especially on mint or unused items.

The fourth option is to store them as the stamp dealers do–in a small glassine envelope that contains only one set, labeled with country, year and reference number. A 3 1/2-inch by 2 1/4-inch glassine works fine. It will protect the stamps and is inexpensive–glassines can be bought in sets of 100 from most stamp stores. You can see the set of stamps through the envelope and also handle them safely. An index card file with alphabetic separators helps to file them (almost) by country. Even when this is not the final way you will store and display your items, it is handy for the interim.

Catalogs

Stamp collecting is a hobby almost as old as postage stamps themselves. To get stamps to collectors, early stamp dealers would publish lists of the items available for sale. Next they added the prices of items to the lists. This then expanded to become a listing of all the items issued by particular countries so dealers could know what stamps to find for interested collectors, even when they were not immediately in stock. Thus was born the modern-stamp catalog.

Nowadays, the stamp catalog is a reference book, since the publisher no longer sells the items listed in there.

Some of the major contemporary world-wide stamp catalogs are:

- Scott's Standard Postage Stamp Catalog, produced in the U.S.
- Stanley Gibbons Stamp Catalog, produced in Great Britain.
- Michel's, an extensive catalog from Germany written in German, with volumes on worldwide stamps, plus very detailed ones for Germany.

These catalogs are all world wide in scope and contain similar information about the philatelic and historical features of the stamps.

There are many other major catalogs for specific countries or regional areas. Some of the more common are:

- Yvert & Tellier, a French catalog.
- Zumstein, a Swiss-produced catalog covering only Europe.
- Facit, a Swedish catalog.
- Others for Japan, Russia and Scandinavia.

Most catalogs illustrate only part of a set. When the shapes are all the same, the catalog usually illustrates only the first item in a set. When the shapes vary within the set, the catalog often shows only the first item in each different shape. Each of these design series has a designator that appears in the list of denominations so you can tell which of the items belong in which design set. When a design reappears in a later issue, the catalog will usually refer back to the original design designation and *not* illustrate with another picture.

One of the most important aspects of catalogs is providing a way to refer to specific stamps. Catalogs usually assign a unique number to each stamp in it. The identification number is a convenient shorthand for referring to the specific item. You use it when ordering stamps from dealers, looking up stamps available on dealer's published lists and keeping track of the items you have and the items you want. The standardization is invaluable for efficient and accurate communication among stamp enthusiasts. However, it does mean one needs access to the catalog where the numbering originates. Without the catalog or some other reference, which defines the item to the numbering scheme, the shorthand numbering has no value.

Here are a few pointers specifically about the Scott catalogs, which can be awkward for the triangular collector:

A) The catalogs are a multi-volume set, with the countries separated into two groupings. USA, British Commonwealth and United Nations make up one group. The rest of the countries make up the second group. In the first group, the countries are not in alphabetical order; in the second group, they are.

B) Within a specific country, Scott organizes the listings by the type of postage stamp. It uses a prefix letter to denote the type of service and sequential numbers within each type— so the prefix letter is *very* important to use. For example, #10, #B10 and #C10 for the same country are three different stamps. Their prefix letters are:

Prefix	Type of service
none	Regular mail
B	Semi-postal
C	Air post
CB	Air post semi-postal
CO	Air post official
E	Special delivery
EX	Personal delivery
F	Registered
J	Postage due
O	Official
P	Newspaper
Q	Parcel post
QE	Special handling
RA	Postal tax
RAB	Postal tax semi-postal

Within each of these types, the stamps are in order by the date of issuance. This creates awkward listings for countries that issue regular postage and air mail in the same set. The Scott catalog lists these items split into type and sometimes separated by more than 60 pages. (Many catalogs organize each country into strictly an issue-date order.)

C) Scott catalogs often use their footnotes to indicate when imperforated separations occurred along with the (primary) perforated separations. Other catalogs often have the separation differences indicated more clearly and completely.)

Access to a standard world-wide general stamp catalog is essential. Public libraries and stamp clubs usually have a set of recent catalogs you can use or borrow. For most work, the catalog can be an older one—prices may have changed and recent items will not be included, but that will happen over time with a new catalog anyway. Stamp clubs, libraries and used-book stores are good sources for buying copies of old catalogs.

A specialization list

When you have defined your collection, you will be able to find or create a list of stamps you eventually expect to have. I recommend you have such a list. It will change over time, but it will be invaluable in communicating with dealers and other collectors.

When you have decided to collect triangulars, and I sincerely hope you have, then this handbook will serve as your "list." If you are a collector of a particular country, standard or specialized stamp catalogs for that country may be your "list." If you are a topical collector, the American Topical Association may have a list that fits how you have defined your collection. Otherwise, you will need to use various sources to develop your own list. Whatever the list you use, expect it will change as you develop more knowledge of your collecting area. You will run across new items to add, and may find reasons to remove some items.

Your initial list actually has two main parts–a list of the stamps you already have, and a list of the stamps you are still seeking. As you acquire items, the entries in your lists move from the "have-not" to the "have" list.

When seeking stamps, you will find an item you do not recognize and will then need to check to see if you already have it or if it is one you actually need. One reason you might not recognize individual stamps is because they are sold and bought in sets. The catalogs usually illustrate only one stamp out of a set, unless the design or format is different from stamp to stamp. And when you buy a set, there will usually be one stamp on top of the set that shows completely. Other items in the set, even though you have them, and particularly when you have not put them in an album, may later appear as strangers to you. An accurate list will help you resolve these uncertainties.

Chapter 7

On Safari–Finding Your Quarry

Now that you have an idea of what you are collecting, how do you go about finding stamps to buy and what to pay for them? This chapter explores many ways for obtaining stamps. One or more of them will fit your own particular circumstances. Triangulars are not very common after you find the most common items–so follow the guidelines presented here. Persevere, do not become discouraged, and you will continue to add items.

Sources for stamps

Once you have decided you would like to collect triangulars, how do you go about finding them? There are several ways you can succeed in your endeavor–but it will take searching. Since most of the major postal-using countries do not issue triangular stamps, you will not find them on a letter from Uncle Sam, or Grandma Liz, or Cousin Bono. You will not find them at your local post office. Unless you live in a really large city, you will not find many at your local stamp dealer, if there even is one in your town. Regardless of where you live, when you follow the guidelines described below, you will find the stamps you seek.

There are five different ways for getting triangular stamps:

- Attending a stamp bourse (a stamp show)
- Going to a stamp store
- Ordering from dealers by phone or mail
- Participating in stamp auctions
- Taking part in a stamp club

The following pages explore each of these in depth. You can pick and choose which activity will work best for you in your particular circumstances and location.

However, before looking at the sources, let us examine some general guidelines for getting triangular stamps. These guidelines apply no matter which source(s) you use.

You will probably be unsuccessful when you ask a dealer for a packet of triangular stamps. Most dealers do not keep their material sorted into triangulars, and they are not likely to know what material they have that is triangular shaped. They need a "want list" of the items you desire.

Here is a key point when working with a stamp dealer: Most dealers will not accurately remember whether they have any triangular stamps. They may remember some key ones, either because they are very common or very expensive, so it is important you ask for the specific items you want. This handbook lets you do that.

The dealers will have their stock identified by one of the standard catalog's reference numbers. In the U.S., dealers use the Scott-numbering system. Great Britain uses the Stanley Gibbons catalog numbering.

When a dealer sells to "topical" collectors, it makes your searching a little more complicated. A topical collector is one who collects stamps on a particular subject, rather than a particular country. There are more than 150 recognized topical topics. There is even a large association oriented toward this type of collecting, the American Topical Association.

When working with a dealer who arranges material by topic, you will often find the items within the topic are *not* kept in any particular order. The country and a standard catalog number are usually indicated. But when they are not filed by country and in number order, you then have to go through the items one-by-one looking for triangular items. This is especially true when searching for Cinderella material. Remember how the triangular shape was first used to permit easy recognition of a "different" stamp? Well, now you can use that feature to quickly recognize the triangular from amongst lots of non-triangular shaped items.

To make working with topically organized material easier, *Triangular Philatelics* provides the relevant topic for stamps in the postage stamp listings. This will greatly assist you in knowing what topic to search in, such as in "flowers," "scouts," "ships," etc.

When dealers have some material arranged by country and some by topic, you will need to look through both groupings.

Attending bourses

Your best initial source for new material will be the stamp bourse, or stamp show. A bourse is a get-together of dealers and collectors to buy, sell, or trade stamps. Cities all over the country have bourses many times throughout the year. They may range from a small one of five dealers, to a medium-sized one of 25-30 dealers or a large one of 100 dealers or more. The medium-sized ones are fairly widespread across the country. It has been my experience that they will have some of the triangular material you seek until your collection gets about 80% complete, and then it gets a lot harder to find the remaining items. Since the same dealers tend to frequent the same bourse circuits, this source for material will eventually become barren for you. The dealers get new stock all the time, but there is a certain similarity to what they tend to acquire. Different dealers have different material due to their different sources and areas of specialty.

For many dealers, selling on the bourse circuit is their livelihood. Each weekend they are "on the road," selling from the stock they acquire and getting ready for selling in between the travel. Some of the dealers will actually span the U.S. continent in the bourses they attend.

Bourses arise in three main ways. First, there are people whose business is to establish, arrange and conduct the bourse. They make all the arrangements, advertise the bourse and charge the dealers for attending. There usually is no admission fee to the collector.

Other bourse "sponsors" are chapters of the American Stamp Dealers Association. These bourses, held in major cities, include dealers who are members of the chapter.

A third type of bourse sponsor is the local stamp club, which will typically sponsor one show each year. These will vary in size and quality of the dealers participating. Some of these shows are very prestigious national or regional events. Some have dealers who sell at only the one bourse during the year–the rest of the time they are doing mail order or they have a retail store. The large ones may attract dealers from around the country, whereas the smaller ones will have local dealers.

To find out what bourse opportunities are in your geographic area, review the philatelic periodicals or contact local stamp clubs for information. When working with bourse dealers, ask them what other bourses they attend. In this way, you will soon build up information on the bourse scene in your area. Keep a file of the information you gather, since the bourses repeat themselves at roughly the same time each year.

Here is a key point for those who travel when you take a vacation: Plan your vacation timing so you can attend a bourse in a different location from where you live. In this way, you will get different dealers with different stock, and thus different material to search. Plan to attend for at least some part of one of the bourse's days.

When you travel on business, check out whether staying over on a Saturday will give you access to a bourse in the area you are visiting–a great way to get a personal bonus from the business trip.

Stamp stores

Be sure to explore the opportunities with all your local stamp stores and ones in any city you happen to visit. Your success will be greater in stores that deal in a range of different countries. They may not be a complete world-wide dealer, but when they specialize in non-U.S., non-British Commonwealth countries, you have an opportunity to fill some of your want list. When they cannot provide items directly, they may be able to provide you with information on where else to try–do not be afraid to ask.

Your local stamp store is also a good source for general philatelic supplies and knowledge.

Many stores have their own auctions. Occasionally, these can be a source of items and often at very good prices. Be sure the store knows who you are, how to contact you and what type of items you are collecting so it can let you know when it gets new items that match your interests.

Working with dealers at a distance

Conducting your search via mail and phone calls is a very valid approach for finding additional items. Unfortunately, it lacks personal contact that can often provide additional bits of information, thus adding to the value from the searching. However, it does have the advantage of being able to reach far more dealers over a wider, even an international distance, as you expand your search to harder-to-find items.

How do you shop for stamps by mail? First, you identify a dealer likely to have items you want. Then write, or call and write, to let them know what you are seeking. This might be particular items, a general list, a general area or a specific order when they have advertised something you want. The dealer will usually put together a packet of the materials or type of material you have requested. They will send this packet to you "on approval," which means you are not obligated to buy the items. The dealer will indicate the price for each item. You usually have 10 days to decide which items to buy and which to return. Many dealers give a discount for buying the whole packet. After deciding, you send them the money for the items you are keeping, and return any items you are not buying.

The want list you send a dealer should indicate whether you desire mint, used, or items in either condition. Use standard-catalog numbers where you can, since it is easier for the dealer to work with that shorthand identifier. Be sure to tell the dealer what catalog(s) you are using. When you have a maximum amount for an order, or for any stamp, be sure to indicate this to the dealer so you are not surprised by items outside your financial resources. You also do not want the expense of sending back a large-dollar packet.

Here are a couple of finer details on this process: Dealers usually pay for postal insurance on items they send, unless the items total a very small amount. When you return items, you will also have to consider getting insurance for them. Insuring them involves an extra cost to the transaction and a trip to the post office, but it protects you in case of their loss in the return mailing.

Now that you understand how the mail-ordering process works, how do you find out what dealers are waiting for your order? The best place is to look in the philatelic periodicals for advertisements from dealers that indicate material similar to what you are seeking. Although dealers may advertise an item you need, realize they are not advertising all they have, but just the most popular items or their overstocked material. A specific ad is unlikely to indicate the triangles you want. What you are seeking is a dealer who handles the countries and age of material you want.

When doing mail order, be sure you do not ask for the same item from more than one dealer at the same time, or you may receive multiple copies. When you return the mutiples, this becomes an annoyance to the dealer, who has to restock them. Be wary about sending your complete want list to several dealers at the same time; possibly split the list into sections. In any case, be sure you clearly state to the dealer how long he has to work on finding items on the list.

Be sure in your initial correspondence to indicate what you are collecting so the dealer can see how he/she can help you. Be sure to mention where you found his name, since that helps him in determining how to operate his business. When you are ordering specific items, but also want approvals sent, be sure to indicate that. Do *not* assume the dealer will automatically send approvals. You have to specify whether you want them.

When you have a limit for how much you can spend at any time, let the dealer know. Tell him not to send you more than that amount. You may also want to request the dealer send you both lower- and higher-priced items from your want list. Otherwise, you may end up with only a few higher-priced items, since that is easier and more profitable for the dealer.

Most dealers have a minimum dollar amount they like per order, since they have time involved to process your order. When a sufficient amount is not forthcoming, it is not profitable for them to handle the order. Realize your order involves them handling it at least three times—processing your initial request, sending the items to you and processing the money or returned items. Be sure your want list has sufficient material so it is worth processing.

When you run across an old advertisement for an item you want, assuming it was not an auction, do not be dismayed by the age of the ad. It is possible to find both a dealer and an advertised item even 10 years after the ad originated—of course, the price may have changed.

Auctions

Stamp auctions are an alternative way of obtaining stamps. It is not suited to the beginning collector, nor to one who is just starting a collection. Most auction material is either large batches of stamps, which might include a few triangles, or higher-priced sets or items. Auctions are a slower way to obtain items, since those that have the material you are seeking are infrequent—and then you will not be the successful bidder, unless you are willing to pay more than anyone else. It is a good method when looking for elusive, higher priced or specialized items. I believe auctions are most useful in helping to complete the collection after extensive use of bourses and approval dealers.

Philatelic publications advertise upcoming auctions. Start by getting some of the free catalogs first and try a few auctions to get a feel for the process. Getting a prices-realized list is also helpful. This lets you gauge for a particular auction house how much it takes to have a winning bid. Many, but not all, major auction houses charge for their catalogs.

One of the modern enhancements in the auctioning process is the use of the touch-tone telephone to check on lots, place bids, check on the bids and find out if you are successful. Several auction houses have excellent phone-bid systems, and even run a large number of auctions only by mail and phone, without any floor bidding.

Another advantage is to discuss the auction process with other serious collectors who have experience dealing with different auction houses.

A good overall perspective on auctions and how they work is found in *Linn's World Stamp Almanac* in the chapter on how to buy and sell stamps.

Stamp clubs

Many cities and towns have stamp clubs—groups of collectors who get together periodically to swap stamps, discuss their latest finds, share information on all aspects of philately and generally have a good time. Also, the larger and older clubs tend to have libraries of philatelic books. Find out what stamp clubs exist in your locale, where and when they meet and then avail yourself of their opportunities. Local stamp dealers will know what clubs are in your area and can put you in contact with someone.

Although the club is not a likely source for many triangular stamps, it is likely a good source of information on the local philatelic scene and general knowledge about philately.

Finding out who, where and what

Having sufficient information is a necessary part of the collecting process. You will need to know:

- What dealers have material in what areas
- What stamp bourses are upcoming
- What auctions are available
- The prices at which items are sold
- What new stamps are being issued

Consult philatelic periodicals to get up-to-date information. These are magazines and newspapers issued monthly or weekly. They contain a great deal of advertisements, but that has two advantages: it helps keep their cost down; and you want the advertisements to find dealer contacts, bourse particulars and stamp information.

Among the most notable periodicals in the USA related to general stamp collecting are the following:

American Philatelist (The) –The monthly journal of the American Philatelic Society. It contains in-depth articles, some advertisements and information related to APS activities. Each issue is around 100 pages, with each page being printed on glossy paper–a true magazine.

Global Stamp News–A weekly newspaper "magazine" that has around 110 pages in each issue. It has primarily articles and advertisements.

Linn's Stamp News–Another weekly newspaper with content like a magazine. Each issue has about 80 pages. It brings information on all aspects of the current scene, articles on aspects of philately and advertisements galore.

Scott Stamp Monthly–A monthly magazine of about 75 pages with comprehensive information on worldwide new issues.

Stamp Collector–A weekly newspaper. Each issue is around 30 pages.

Stamps–Another weekly newspaper "magazine." Each issue is around 30 pages.

You may find these at a magazine store, your local public library or you can get a subscription from the publishers.

Other countries will have their own publications with similar information.

Another source of dealer names and addresses are the directories put out by different philatelic publishers. *Linn's Stamp News* publishes an annual *Yellow Pages for Stamp Collectors* around mid-year. It has more than 300 philatelic topics with names, addresses and (usually) phone numbers of dealers in each topic. In the spring, *Linn's* publishes a *North American Stamp Store Directory*. This is a listing in state and city order of retail stamp outlets. The American Philatelic Society publishes the *APS Handbook* that contains two extensive dealer listings–one in alphabetical order and one in geographical order. The alphabetical listing indicates the dealers' areas of business specialty. *Stamp Collector* issues an annual *Who's Who In the Philatelic World*, but there are a limited number of dealers included–it is a supplement of advertisements rather than a true directory.

When the above-mentioned directories are unavailable, try the telephone company's "Yellow Pages" for cities all across the USA. Public libraries often have extensive sets of these–nowadays, typically on microfiche covering a huge number of U.S. cities.

Bourses have mailing lists, so once you have attended and signed in or registered for the "hourly drawing for a free prize," you will get notification of future bourses.

To buy or not to buy

That is the question when you find a stamp priced high relative to catalog values; find a complete set when you only need one item from it; or find a needed stamp in poor condition.

What to pay for an item? It is sometimes difficult to arrive at an answer to this question. There are two parts to this decision: the price set by the seller, and the desire you, as a buyer, have for owning the item.

The stamps in the major postage-stamp catalogs are "priced." This price is a guideline for an actual stamp's price. Some dealers sell at the catalog price, and some sell at a 20%-30% discount from the catalog. Dealer's advertised prices and auction prices realized are probably a more accurate guide.

The price reflects two forces at work–the available supply of the item, and the demand that exists for it. Some stamps are high priced because many collectors are seeking one from a limited supply. Other items that may have far fewer available may not cost as much because there are less people wanting to obtain one.

We are seeing more and more of an international influence on setting prices. This arises since long-distance communications, delivery of items and payment are now so easy to most places in the world. Paying for an item with a charge card accommodates the currency differences between countries and there is little surcharge to either seller or buyer.

You need to consider the overall quality of an item when evaluating its price, particularly when it is a high-priced item. Factors influencing the quality are:

- How well it has been preserved
- How "accurately" it was originally produced, like in the centering of the design within the paper space
- How "nicely" it has been canceled when it is a used item
- How significant the cancellation may be, like when and where it was postally used
- The quality of the perforations, especially at the corners
- When it is an imperf, whether the borders are full (very desirable), or whether the design has been cut into (very undesirable)
- Whether the item is dirty, has thins or has tears.

The better the quality, the higher the price one can expect to pay.

The cornerstone to buying at a good price starts with being informed about the items. The current major catalogs provide specific pricing guidelines for postage stamps. Use a fairly recent catalog, since periodically stamp prices change, both increasing and decreasing, as a response to supply-and-demand factors. For the majority of Cinderella stamps, there is no "catalog" pricing to use as a guide. The catalogs are only a guide and your individual experiences may vary considerably one way or the other, so be prepared to delight when paying far less than you had planned, and to pass up items when the price is far more than you want to pay.

Ultimately, what you pay for an item may depend on how badly you want it. When you have been searching for a key item for, say, a year or more, you are probably willing to pay a premium. Whereas, when there are several copies of one item available at different dealers, or even with the same dealer, you will not want to pay even the initial asking price. The dealer's prices are only as firm as that dealer wants or needs at that time. When a dealer has an overstock of a particular item, the negotiation of a discount is more likely.

At some point, you will need to consider whether to buy only complete sets or whether it is appropriate to buy a partial set or an individual item. Remember that most postage stamps exist in sets. Most dealers stock and sell postage stamps as sets, particularly when they are mint stamps. So what do you do when you find an item or a couple you need that are not a complete set? Or when the dealer wants to sell a complete set, of which only some are triangles? A sound consideration here is how much the items are going to cost and how easily you can get back to the dealer if you do not get them now. When the cost is not too great, buy them. When they are a partial set, try to fill it; but when you run across the complete set, then buy it. Sometimes dealers will split a set, especially when you are willing to pay a premium for the item(s) you want.

When you decide not to take an item, be sure to keep good notes about where you found it and for how much—one way is to get a business card from the dealer and make notes on the back. This may become relevant later when you find the rest of the set with a different dealer—then you can buy from each dealer and assemble the complete set.

Cinderellas are a completely different story when it comes to sets; rarely do they come as complete sets. You can expect to buy them an item or two at a time and slowly over time build to having a complete set, if you even know what a complete set is. Many of the "sets" listed in the Cinderella section may actually be an incomplete listing, so be careful that does not lead you to miss looking for additional items. (This warning also holds true for postage stamps, but there you are far less likely to find an unlisted item.)

Chapter 8

After the Hunt

Now that you have obtained some nice triangular stamps, there are still some important tasks to accomplish. This includes making sure of the identity of the stamps–dealers do get them mis-identified. You also will need to store them in a way that is pleasing to you as the collector, and also protective of the stamps themselves. Finally, you will need to have, and keep current, some type of recordkeeping of what you have obtained; otherwise, you will end up buying duplicate items. This chapter gives you guidance in each of these three important areas.

Identifying and storing your stamps

Identifying the stamps you find is a necessary step of collecting. You will want a proper identification for all your items. If you obtained them without the country and/or a reference number, you may have a real challenge.

The steps for successfully identifying a postage stamp will typically include the following, and in this order:

- First, determine the country.
- Secondly, determine the year of issuance. In some cases, the stamp has a date printed on it. Otherwise, match the style of the stamp and the design with a catalog reference. Also, the denomination of the stamp may help in locating the approximate time period of its issuance.
- Then, consider any special printed markings such as surcharges or overprints. These may place the stamp in a completely different classification than one without the special markings.
- Use the above determined information and a catalog to check the catalog's descriptions for the colors and denominations for all the items in a set.
- Finally, check any footnotes under the catalog listing you believe is for the stamp. These footnotes will often refer to other items using the same design. Check these out since you may find a better (the correct) match to your item.

This should provide you with a single catalog reference number for the stamp.

Using this handbook will narrow your search tremendously. For postage stamps, the listings in the next chapter, plus an illustrated worldwide stamp catalog, will point you to the triangular items issued. Using the country-year-type-of-stamp information will let you quickly identify your triangular postage stamps.

For Cinderella items, this handbook will be an enormous assist. The detailed descriptions, selected illustrations and broad scope of the information included will provide a way for identifying most items. Chapter 12 is a Triangular Cinderella Finder provided to help you find entries in the listing that match an item you are trying to identify. It is an index to the listings. However, it will not always provide the desired identification, since there are triangular Cinderella items not included herein. When you find an item you can not identify, you can use a service I provide as indicated in the Afterword.Now that you have succeeded in finding lots of lovely triangular items, what do you do with them?

The section on Storage and Display discusses the alternatives for storing your stamps. I will assume you have explored those alternatives and chosen at least one. You now have two important steps to accomplish, and maybe your actions will get them done at the same time. Organize your material so you know which items you have and be sure to store and protect them.

One protective measure for the stamps is to use stamp tongs. *Do not* use your fingers when handling stamps. Fingers may leave an acidic residue. Stamp tongs are inexpensive and after some practice will be an easy way for handling your stamps (see the tools section in Chapter 6). Whatever method you choose for storing your stamps, be sure to store them vertically. This will be less damaging to them over time.

Logging your stamps

One of the most important things to do after acquiring new stamps is to record them in your "stamp log." The stamp log is where you keep track of which ones you have, where you got them, what you paid for them and any other information that may help find other stamps in the future.

Initially, you will probably expect you can remember which items you have; and that where you got them and what you paid is not important. *Wrong!* As you continue with your collecting, you will not accurately remember or recognize whether you have an item. You may recognize the stamp due to having seen it in someone else's collection, a display, a catalog or even as one of the illustrations in this handbook. And later you will want to re-contact particular dealers already useful in your searches–this may be after a year or more, so accurate records will help. Knowing what you pay for the items helps in developing a sense of what appropriate prices are for similar material, particularly in the Cinderella area where there is little current pricing information published.

You can use this handbook as a log. There are "check-off" boxes provided so you can easily record what you have obtained–either by a check mark or putting the price in the appropriate box. *Use this feature.* Check items off as you buy them to keep your records up to date. This is really important when you are at a stamp show or bourse. Then, as a double check, later at home go back through the day's purchases and be sure they were all checked off in the right box. It is very disheartening to learn some months later, after exhaustively searching your storage and working area, that a set you checked off is one you do not actually have and have not been seeking. It is not quite so bad to buy something and then find out you already had the set, since now you have a duplicate set and can trade with someone at a stamp club for something you need.

Use one of the standard catalogs to research more about an item when you are not sure which one it is–and be aware that dealers sometimes get their identification of the items wrong. It is very disheartening to later discover you have checked off an item you really do not have, since you may have passed up many one-time opportunities to obtain it.

Computerized help

Nowdays, so many American households have personal computers, that it is appropriate to consider their role in helping the collector. For those who already have a computer and are comfortable using it in new ways, there is an opportunity for your consideration. For those without a computer, let me assure you that stamp collecting works just fine without its help.

The computer is very powerful for keeping track of data and assisting you in organizing it. There is quite a quantity of data associated with triangular philatelics, and even more so when you are collecting Cinderellas, as well as regular stamps. A spreadsheet or database will provide a way for keeping the data readily available and useful. Consider how useful an up-to-date computer list can be for preparing want lists, letters to dealers and all of the logging activities you want to do. However, the computer's help is only as useful as the data you entered and the completeness of that entry. When you do not keep it current with your collection, it will become a burden more than a help since you will not be able to rely on its content. Keep it current and you will have a great assistant.

The philatelic journals have many ads for different specialized philatelic computer software. Alternatively, a general purpose spreadsheet program, like EXCEL or LOTUS 123, will work just fine. If you are an advanced computer user, an actual database program may be an advantage.

Chapter 9

Postage-Stamp Listing

The listing sections of this handbook will help you know what is available for collecting; provide information about interesting aspects of particular stamps; and permit logging your personal collection.

The listings first separate the philatelic items into five major groups:

- Postage stamps–1853 through 1996
- Diagonally perforated bisects
- Postal stationery
- Souvenir sheets
- Triangular stamps-on-stamps

Each group is arranged alphabetically by country. For each country, the items are listed by year of issue, and then by type of mail service. When a set was issued with more than one type of separation, they appear as separate listing entries.

This handbook is intended for use with a major worldwide catalog, like Scott's, to find more specific details about the stamps–such as the perforation count, size, design, denominations, colors, and expected market pricing. This listing provides a way to know what items to look for and does not duplicate information readily available elsewhere.

The columns of information are:

Catalog number–This column is provided for you to complete. Use the standard illustrated worldwide reference guide used by the majority of stamp dealers in your country. For example, in the U.S., use the Scott Publishing catalogs; in Great Britain and former commonwealth countries, use the Stanley Gibbon's catalogs; in Germany, use the Michel catalogs; etc. With the information on the country, year, type of mail service, number in set, topic, and your catalog's illustrations, it is quite easy to find each of the entries in the listing. Identify the relevant catalog numbers for each set and clearly write them into the "Catalog Number" column. Do this at your local stamp dealers or library. The catalogs do not have to be the latest issue. You might also want to jot down the set or item price at the same time. For items not listed in the Scott Publishing catalogs, a Michel number is already provided and indicated as m { }.

Number in set–The listing provides the number of triangular items and the total number of items in a set. When the set is all triangular, only one number is stated. When the set contains other shapes, the number of triangles comes first, then /, then the total number in the set. For example, 4/6 indicates 4 triangulars in a set of 6 items.

Separation type–The kind of separation is indicated: "imperf" is for an imperforate stamp; "perf" is for a stamp that has been perforated; and "rouletted" is for one that has roulette separations.

Check-off boxes–These are provided for you to use to record the items you obtain and their condition.

Topic–This column indicates where to look when working with dealers who have their stock arranged topically.

To assist you in evaluating the potential scarcity of a particular stamp, there is an annotation when the quantity issued was less than 10,000.

The listings exclude proofs, essays and errors.

Postage stamps–1853 through 1996

AFGHANISTAN

1952	Regular Mail	2	imperf	U.N.
1952	Regular Mail	2	perf	U.N.
1960	Semi-Postal	2	imperf	U.N.
1960	Semi-Postal	2	perf	
1964	Regular Mail	7	mixed	

This issue has four perf items and three imperf items. The two low value denominations are in both forms; two of the mid-value items are the other imperf. Only 6,000 sets.

ALBANIA

1973	Regular Mail	8	perf	flowers

These eight items were printed se-tenant and a block of eight stamps can have all eight different designs and denominations. However, there is also a label that can be in a block of eight instead of the 30-q denomination stamp. This probably occurs once for every four sets of eight items. See the Cinderella stamp listings for more information on this tab.

ASCENSION

1973	Regular Mail	3	perf	animals

AUSTRALIA

These are the first self-adhesive triangulars. They were issued in sheets of 20 from a bank's ATM (Automatic Teller Machine).

1994	Regular Mail	8	imperf	

AUSTRIA

1916	Special Handling	2	imperf	
1916	Special Handling	2	perf	

These special handling issues were the first triangulars to have the apex of the stamp at the bottom of the design's orientation.

BANGLADESH

1984	Regular Mail	2	perf	stamp collecting

This is one of very few triangular stamps where the long side of the triangle is *not* horizontal when viewing the design in its proper orientation. The triangle is "sitting" on its side rather than on its base or apex. There is also a souvenir sheet.

Year	Type of Mail Service	Catalog No.	No. in set	Separation Type	Check-off boxes Mint CTO Used Cover	Topic

BENIN

| 1983 | Regular Mail | | 1 | perf | | |

BHUTAN

1966	Regular Mail		15	imperf		snowman
1966	Regular Mail		15	perf		snowman
1968	Regular Mail		8	imperf		Olympics
1968	Regular Mail		8	perf		Olympics

Each of the 1968 sets has four denominations with two different overprints on each denomination.

| 1970 | Regular Mail | | 4/19 | perf | | snowman |
| 1970 | Regular Mail | | 2/23 | perf | | snowman |

BOLIVIA

1931	Regular Mail		2	perf		
1931	Postage Due		6	perf		
1937	Regular Mail		2/8	perf		
1938	Postage Due		3	perf		
1939	Air Post		2/10	perf		
1952	Regular Mail		3	perf		
1952	Air Post		4	perf		
1952	Air Post		1	imperf		

BRAZIL

This stamp was required for mailings within Brazil during the week of November 15-22, 1947 to commemorate Aviation Week. On the stamp the 40 cts is the amount for the postage (appearing on the left of the design), while the 10 cts is the amount of the tax. There is also a variation in which the word "CORREIO" has been misprinted as "CURREIO."

| 1947 | Post Tax Semi-Post | | 1 | perf | | |

BRUNEI

This is an example of an overprint that changed the year printed on the stamp. The "1967" was blocked out with four short bars and "1968" was added. The stamp was issued only with the overprint.

| 1968 | Regular Mail | | 1/3 | perf | | |

CAMEROUN

The printing of these stamps was done in tete beche, se-tenant pairs for each denomination. This means the designs are upside down relative to each other and the designs are different on each stamp of the pair.

| 1963 | Postage Due | | 16 | perf | | flowers |

CAPE OF GOOD HOPE

Although there were 12 basic triangular stamps issued by the Cape from 1853 through 1864, there were also many color variations and reprints produced. There also have been numerous forgeries. Since most of these stamps are very expensive, it is advisable before acquiring items to do some in-depth study of the "Capes" to be sure of what you are purchasing.

Year	Type of Mail Service	No. in set	Separation Type
1853	Regular Mail	2	imperf
1855	Regular Mail	4	imperf
1861	Regular Mail	2	imperf
1863	Regular Mail	4	imperf

CENTRAL AFRICA

Year	Type of Mail Service	No. in set	Separation Type	Topic
1962	Postage Due	12	perf	beetles
1985	Postage Due	3	perf	animals

CHAD

Year	Type of Mail Service	No. in set	Separation Type	Topic
1962	Postage Due	12	perf	animals

CHINA, PEOPLE'S REPUBLIC OF

Year	Type of Mail Service	No. in set	Separation Type	Topic
1951	Regular Mail	3	perf	birds

Warning: A reprint of this set is very common and readily available.

COLOMBIA

Year	Type of Mail Service	No. in set	Separation Type
1865	Regular Mail	1/8	imperf
1869	Regular Mail	1	imperf

This is the only postage stamp that is a scalene triangle.

Year	Type of Mail Service	No. in set	Separation Type
1969	Air Post	1	perf
1987	Special Delivery	2	perf

CONGO PEOPLE'S REPUBLIC

Year	Type of Mail Service	No. in set	Separation Type	Topic
1961	Postage Due	12	perf	transportation

COOK ISLANDS

The 10 items consist of two stamps with different designs for each of five denominations. They were issued in sheets of 10 with two of the same denomination printed se-tenant. The issue also includes a souvenir sheet of 12 items: the 10 different stamps and two labels.

Year	Type of Mail Service	No. in set	Separation Type
1969	Regular Mail	10	perf

COSTA RICA

Year	Type of Mail Service	Catalog No.	No. in set	Separation Type	Mint	CTO	Used	Cover	Topic
1932	Regular Mail		4	perf					philately
1937	Regular Mail		4	perf					philately
1937	Regular Mail		1/5	perf					fish

There is also a souvenir sheet.

Year	Type of Mail Service	Catalog No.	No. in set	Separation Type	Mint	CTO	Used	Cover	Topic
1963	Air Post		8	perf					animals
1963	Air Post		4	perf					animals

This set has a surcharge on the printed values. They were printed with 1 to 4 centavos. As printed, they were never issued. The airmail rate was 25 centavos and the increment between rates was 10 centavos. Rather than disposing of unused stamps, they repriced (surcharged) them with rates starting at 25 centavos.

CUBA

Year	Type of Mail Service	Catalog No.	No. in set	Separation Type	Mint	CTO	Used	Cover	Topic
1959	Semi-Postal		1	imperf					
1959	Semi-Postal		1	perf					
1975	Regular Mail		3	perf					minerals
1996	Regular Mail		1	perf					

CZECHOSLOVAKIA-BOHEMIA and MORAVIA

Year	Type of Mail Service	Catalog No.	No. in set	Separation Type	Mint	CTO	Used	Cover	Topic
1939	Personal delivery		2	perf					

CZECHOSLOVAKIA-SLOVAKIA

Year	Type of Mail Service	Catalog No.	No. in set	Separation Type	Mint	CTO	Used	Cover	Topic
1940	Personal delivery		2	imperf					

CZECHOSLOVAKIA

Year	Type of Mail Service	Catalog No.	No. in set	Separation Type	Mint	CTO	Used	Cover	Topic
1919	Semi-Postal		2	perf					250 copies of B33
1937	Personal Delivery		2	perf					
1946	Personal Delivery		1	perf					

DAHOMEY

Year	Type of Mail Service	Catalog No.	No. in set	Separation Type	Mint	CTO	Used	Cover	Topic
1967	Postage Due		10	perf					communications

DOMINICAN REPUBLIC

Year	Type of Mail Service	Catalog No.	No. in set	Separation Type	Mint	CTO	Used	Cover	Topic
1935	Regular Mail		1/4	perf					
1936	Regular Mail		1/13	perf					
1939	Air Post		1	perf					airplanes
1957	Regular Mail		5	imperf					Olympics
1957	Regular Mail		5	perf					Olympics

Year	Type of Mail Service	Catalog No.	No. in set	Separation Type	Check-off boxes				Topic
					Mint	CTO	Used	Cover	

The 1957 Regular Mail issue has two mini-sheets, each with the five stamps of this issue. In one sheet the stamps are perforated, and in the other they are imperforate.

| 1957 | Air Post | 3 | imperf | | | | | Olympics |
| 1957 | Air Post | 3 | perf | | | | | Olympics |

This issue has two mini-sheets, each with the three stamps of this issue. In one sheet the stamps are perforated, and in the other they are imperforate.

| 1958 | Semi-Postal | 10 | perf | | | | | Olympics |
| 1958 | Air Post Semi-Postal | 6 | perf | | | | | Olympics |

The 1958 Semi-Postal and 1958 Air Post Semi-Postal issues have eight mini-sheets, each with either the five or three stamps of the 1957 Regular Mail mini-sheets or the 1957 Air Post mini-sheets. Each stamp on the mini-sheets has a +5-cent surcharge (whereas the stamps in these two semi-postal issues have only a +2-cent surcharge). Each surcharge comes in two styles, one with the Star of David and one with a crescent moon. In four sheets the stamps are perforated, and in four they are imperforate. Only 2,500 sets were issued.

| 1960 | Postal Tax | 1 | perf | | | | | |

This was a postal tax for the Anti-tuberculosis League.

ECUADOR

| 1908 | Regular Mail | 5/7 | perf | | | | | |

This issue was the first perforated triangular postage stamp.

| 1936 | Regular Mail | 6 | perf | | | | | |
| 1936 | Air Post | 6 | perf | | | | | |

This airmail set has the same design and denominations as the 1936 Regular Mail issue. However, the color for each denomination is different and they are overprinted with "AEREA." Only 10,000 sets issued.

1956	Air Post	1	perf					U.N.
1957	Air Post	1	perf					U.N.
1959	Air Post	1	perf					U.N.
1964	Air Post	1	perf					U.N.

EGYPT

1962	Regular Mail	6	perf					sports
1963	Semi-Postal	2/3	perf					stamps
1964	Regular Mail	2	perf					scouting
1965	Semi-Postal	3	perf					

EQUATORIAL GUINEA

| 1972 | Regular Mail | 1 | perf | | | | | |

Year	Type of Mail Service	Catalog No.	No. in set	Separation Type	Check-off boxes				Topic
					Mint	CTO	Used	Cover	

ESTONIA

Year	Type of Mail Service	Catalog No.	No. in set	Separation Type	Mint	CTO	Used	Cover	Topic
1920	Air Post		1	imperf					airplanes
1923	Air Post		1	imperf					airplanes
1923	Air Post		1	imperf					airplanes
1923	Air Post		3	imperf					airplanes; 9,900 sets
1923	Air Post		2	perf					airplanes; 300 C7; 2,000 C8
1924	Air Post		5	imperf					airplanes
1925	Air Post		5	perf					airplanes

ETHIOPIA

Year	Type of Mail Service	Catalog No.	No. in set	Separation Type	Mint	CTO	Used	Cover	Topic
1961	Regular Mail		3	perf					
1979	Regular Mail		5	perf					

FINLAND

Year	Type of Mail Service	Catalog No.	No. in set	Separation Type	Mint	CTO	Used	Cover	Topic
1994	Regular Mail		1	perf					insects
1995	Regular Mail		1	perf					insects
1996	Regular Mail		1	perf					insects

FIUME

Year	Type of Mail Service	Catalog No.	No. in set	Separation Type	Mint	CTO	Used	Cover	Topic
1919	Newspaper		2	perf					birds
1920	Newspaper		1	imperf					ships
1920	Newspaper		1	perf					ships

GABON

Year	Type of Mail Service	Catalog No.	No. in set	Separation Type	Mint	CTO	Used	Cover	Topic
1962	Postage Due		12	perf					fruit

GERMAN DEMOCRATIC REPUBLIC

Year	Type of Mail Service	Catalog No.	No. in set	Separation Type	Mint	CTO	Used	Cover	Topic
1964	Semi-Postal		3	perf					

GHANA

Year	Type of Mail Service	Catalog No.	No. in set	Separation Type	Mint	CTO	Used	Cover	Topic
1965	Regular Mail		3/6	perf					

GIBRALTAR

Year	Type of Mail Service	Catalog No.	No. in set	Separation Type	Mint	CTO	Used	Cover	Topic
1975	Regular Mail		3	perf					scouting

GRENADA

Year	Type of Mail Service	Catalog No.	No. in set	Separation Type	Mint	CTO	Used	Cover	Topic
1981	Regular Mail		8	perf					
1997	Regular Mail		6	perf					

These are two self-adhesive sheets, each with three stamps.

Year	Type of Mail Service	Catalog No.	No. in set	Separation Type	Check-off boxes				Topic
					Mint	CTO	Used	Cover	

GUATEMALA

| 1929 | Official | | 7 | perf | | | | | |

HAITI

The Haitian issues are all of the same design with the issues done for four different postal purposes. They were also produced in mini-sheets of 12 of each Regular Mail and Air Post item for a total of six mini-sheets. Also, Michel indicates the six basic stamps may exist imperforate, but I haven't been able to confirm. I also wonder if there are mini-sheets with the surcharging. (Please let me know if you can confirm either.)

1962	Regular Mail		3	perf					
1962	Semi-Postal		3	perf					
1962	Air Post		3	perf					

Souvenir sheets were also issued.

| 1962 | Air Post Semi-Postal | | 3 | perf | | | | | |

HUNGARY

Note that since 1949, Hungary has for many of its stamps issued imperf versions in very small quantities and at greatly increased prices. These were created to get additional money from collectors.

1952	Air Post		11	imperf					birds
1952	Air Post		11	perf					birds
1956	Regular Mail		4/8	perf					dogs
1958	Regular Mail		4/8	imperf					flowers; 3,504 sets
1958	Regular Mail		4/8	perf					flowers

Souvenir sheets were also issued.

1963	Regular Mail		2/3	imperf					transportation; 3,768 sets
1963	Regular Mail		2/3	perf					transportation
1964	Regular Mail		1/18	imperf					3,283 sets
1964	Regular Mail		1/18	perf					
1964	Regular Mail		3	imperf					2,780 sets
1964	Regular Mail		3	perf					
1973	Regular Mail		7	imperf					sports; 5,687 sets
1973	Regular Mail		7	perf					sports
1995	Semi-Postal		2	perf					Olympics

ICELAND

| 1930 | Air Post | | 1 | perf | | | | | birds |
| 1930 | Air Post Official | | 1 | perf | | | | | birds |

Year	Type of Mail Service	Catalog No.	No. in set	Separation Type	Check-off boxes				Topic
					Mint	CTO	Used	Cover	

INDIA

Year	Type of Mail Service	Catalog No.	No. in set	Separation Type	Mint	CTO	Used	Cover	Topic
1985	Regular Mail		1	perf					
1990	Regular Mail		1	perf					

INDIA-BHOPAL

Year	Type of Mail Service	Catalog No.	No. in set	Separation Type	Mint	CTO	Used	Cover	Topic
1935	Official		1	perf					
1937	Official		1	perf					
1939	Official		1	perf					
1941	Official		1	perf					

INDONESIA

Year	Type of Mail Service	Catalog No.	No. in set	Separation Type	Mint	CTO	Used	Cover	Topic
1996	Regular Mail		1	perf					space

IRAQ

Year	Type of Mail Service	Catalog No.	No. in set	Separation Type	Mint	CTO	Used	Cover	Topic
1965	Regular Mail		3	imperf					
1965	Regular Mail		3	perf					
1965	Regular Mail		1	perf					

There is also a souvenir sheet.

Year	Type of Mail Service	Catalog No.	No. in set	Separation Type	Mint	CTO	Used	Cover	Topic
1969	Regular Mail		1	perf					
1970	Regular Mail		2	perf					

IVORY COAST

Year	Type of Mail Service	Catalog No.	No. in set	Separation Type	Mint	CTO	Used	Cover	Topic
1974	Official		4	perf					

JAMAICA

Year	Type of Mail Service	Catalog No.	No. in set	Separation Type	Mint	CTO	Used	Cover	Topic
1964	Regular Mail		1/3	perf					
1965	Regular Mail		1/2	perf					

JORDAN

Year	Type of Mail Service	Catalog No.	No. in set	Separation Type	Mint	CTO	Used	Cover	Topic
1964	Regular Mail		10	perf					space
1964	Regular Mail		6	imperf					Kennedy; 5,400 sets
1964	Regular Mail		6	perf					Kennedy

There is also a souvenir sheet.

Year	Type of Mail Service	Catalog No.	No. in set	Separation Type	Mint	CTO	Used	Cover	Topic
1964	Regular Mail		8	imperf					Olympics; 5,000 sets
1964	Regular Mail	8	perf	Olympics					

There is also a souvenir sheet.

Year	Type of Mail Service	Catalog No.	No. in set	Separation Type	Mint	CTO	Used	Cover	Topic
1964	Regular Mail		7	imperf					scouting
1964	Regular Mail		7	perf					scouting

There is also a souvenir sheet.

Year	Type of Mail Service	Catalog No.	No. in set	Separation Type	Check-off boxes				Topic
					Mint	CTO	Used	Cover	

KENYA

1982	Regular Mail		4	perf					sports

There is also a souvenir sheet.

1987	Regular Mail		5	perf					communication

There is also a souvenir sheet.

KENYA, UGANDA, TANZANIA

1976	Regular Mail		4	perf				

KUWAIT

1964	Regular Mail		4	perf				

LATVIA

1921	Air Post		2	perf					airplanes
1921	Air Post		2	imperf					airplanes
1928	Air Post		3	perf					airplanes
1928	Air Post		1	perf					airplanes
1931	Air Post		3	perf					airplanes
1931	Air Post Semi-Post		3	perf					airplanes
1931	Air Post Semi-Post		3	imperf					airplanes
1932	Air Post Semi-Post		3	perf					birds
1932	Air Post Semi-Post		3	imperf					birds; 7,000 sets
1933	Air Post		5	imperf					airplanes; 2,930 sets
1933	Air Post Semi-Post		3	perf					airplanes
1933	Air Post Semi-Post		3	imperf					airplanes; 8,420 sets

LESOTHO

1967	Regular Mail		3	perf				

LIBERIA

They started issuing CTOs back in 1885 and have ever since. Real used copies are much harder to find.

1894	Regular Mail		1	imperf				
1894	Regular Mail		1	rouletted				
1894	Official		1	imperf				
1894	Official		1	rouletted				
1901	Regular Mail		1	imperf				
1909	Regular Mail		1/10	perf				
1909	Regular Mail		1	rouletted				
1909	Official		1/10	perf				

Year	Type of Mail Service	Catalog No.	No. in set	Separation Type	Check-off boxes				Topic
					Mint	CTO	Used	Cover	
1909	Official	1	rouletted						
1910	Regular Mail	2	rouletted						
1910	Regular Mail	2	perf						
1910	Official	1	rouletted						
1910	Official	1	perf						
1913	Regular Mail	1	perf						
1915	Semi-Postal	2	perf						
1918	Regular Mail	1/13	perf						
1918	Semi-Postal	1	perf						
1918	Official	1	perf						
1918	Official	1/13	perf						
1919	Registered	5	perf						ships
1919	Registered	5	rouletted						ships
1921	Registered	5	perf						snakes
1921	Registered	5	perf						snakes
1936	Regular Mail	1	perf						
1936	Air Post	6	imperf						airplanes
1936	Air Post	6	perf						airplanes
1937	Regular Mail	6	perf						animals
1938	Air Post	2/10	perf						birds
1941	Air Post	2/10	perf						birds
1942	Air Post	2/10	perf						birds
1944	Regular Mail	6/12	perf						animals
1944	Air Post	5/9	perf						birds
1953	Regular Mail	3/6	imperf						birds
1953	Regular Mail	3/6	perf						birds

LIBYA

Year	Type of Mail Service	Catalog No.	No. in set	Separation Type	Topic
1962	Regular Mail		3	imperf	
1962	Regular Mail		3	perf	

There is also a souvenir sheet.

Year	Type of Mail Service	Catalog No.	No. in set	Separation Type	Topic
1966	Regular Mail		3	perf	space
1973	Regular Mail		2	perf	sports

LITHUANIA

Year	Type of Mail Service	Catalog No.	No. in set	Separation Type	Topic
1922	Air Post		6	perf	airplanes

There are three denominations issued in this set, each with its own distinctive colored border. However, there are two varieties for each stamp. In the most common form of the stamps, the border design at the apex (just above the box containing the denomination) has a semicircle and five rays. In the variation, there is a tiny solid semicircle appearing inside the semicircle of the basic stamp; this addition is colored the same as the border. Thus, this issue contains six different items.

Year	Type of Mail Service	Catalog No.	No. in set	Separation Type	Topic
1922	Air Post		1	perf	

Year	Type of Mail Service	Catalog No.	No. in set	Separation Type	Mint	CTO	Used	Cover	Topic
1932	Air Post		8	imperf					
1932	Air Post		8	perf					
1932	Air Post		8	imperf					
1932	Air Post		8	perf					
1932	Air Post		5	perf					500 sets
1933	Air Post		8	imperf					
1933	Air Post		8	perf					
1933	Air Post		8	imperf					
1933	Air Post		8	perf					
1991	Regular Mail		3	perf					

MALAYA

This set is inscribed with, "BAHASA JIWA BANGSA," which is Malay for "language is the life of the nation." This set was issued for its National Language Month.

Year	Type of Mail Service	Catalog No.	No. in set	Separation Type	Mint	CTO	Used	Cover	Topic
1962	Regular Mail		3	perf					

MALAYSIA

Year	Type of Mail Service	Catalog No.	No. in set	Separation Type	Mint	CTO	Used	Cover	Topic
1966	Regular Mail		2	perf					

MALDIVE ISLANDS

Year	Type of Mail Service	Catalog No.	No. in set	Separation Type	Mint	CTO	Used	Cover	Topic
1963	Regular Mail		8	perf					fish

This set was also issued in mini-sheets of eight of each stamp.

Year	Type of Mail Service	Catalog No.	No. in set	Separation Type	Mint	CTO	Used	Cover	Topic
1968	Regular Mail		9	perf					space

There is also a souvenir sheet.

Year	Type of Mail Service	Catalog No.	No. in set	Separation Type	Mint	CTO	Used	Cover	Topic
1975	Regular Mail		8	perf					sea life

There is also a souvenir sheet.

MALI

Year	Type of Mail Service	Catalog No.	No. in set	Separation Type	Mint	CTO	Used	Cover	Topic
1964	Postage Due		14	perf					butterflies
1972	Regular Mail		12	perf					zodiac
1980	Air Post		4	perf					space

This set of Jules Vern space fantasy designs is composed of a stamp plus a tete beche, se-tenant label. The label is a drawing related to the theme of the stamps, but without any text or numbers. It is strictly added decoration. See the section in Cinderellas on se-tenant tabs for more details.

Year	Type of Mail Service	Catalog No.	No. in set	Separation Type	Mint	CTO	Used	Cover	Topic
1984	Postage Due		14	perf					butterflies

MAURITANIA

Year	Type of Mail Service	Catalog No.	No. in set	Separation Type	Mint	CTO	Used	Cover	Topic
1963	Postage Due		16	perf					birds

MONACO

Note: Monaco issued a few imperforate sheets for most of its issues after 1939.

1946	Regular Mail		1/5	perf					Roosevelt
1946	Air Post SemiPost		1/4	perf					Roosevelt
1951	Regular Mail		2/12	perf					
1953	Postage Due		18	perf					ships
1956	Regular Mail		22	perf					transportation
1980	Postage Due		12	perf					
1988	Regular Mail		2	perf					

MONGOLIA

Note that Mongolia has issued CTOs since 1958. Also since these stamps were produced by the Hungarian State Printing Office, there are probably imperfs of the Mongolian items just as was done with the Hungarian issues.

1959	Regular Mail		3/7	perf					animals
1961	Regular Mail		7	perf					birds
1962	Regular Mail		8	perf					fish
1973	Regular Mail		7	perf					birds
1973	Regular Mail		8	perf					animals
1973	Regular Mail		8	perf					flowers
1977	Regular Mail		7	perf					animals
1980	Air Post		7	perf					insects
1984	Regular Mail		7	perf					animals

MOZAMBIQUE

| 1928 | Regular Mail | m{12} | 10 | perf | | | | |
| 1928 | Postal Tax | | 10 | perf | | | | |

In 1928, Mozambique had very few regular issues. Its most recent designs had been issued 14 years earlier. A postal tax set was issued as a way to raise money for the Cross of the Orient Society, a Red Cross agency. It had to be used for all mail on certain days of the year. It used rectangular-shaped stamps for this postal tax for two years before it switched to the triangular shape, probably because the triangular was easier to recognize on those days when it was required postage.

MOZAMBIQUE COMPANY

1935	Regular Mail		10	perf					airplanes
1937	Regular Mail		7/19	perf					animals
1939	Regular Mail		7	perf					animals

NEPAL

1956	Regular Mail		1	perf					U.N.
1966	Regular Mail		1	perf					stamp collecting
1973	Regular Mail		3	perf					

Year	Type of Mail Service	Catalog No.	No. in set	Separation Type	Check-off boxes				Topic
					Mint	CTO	Used	Cover	

NETHERLANDS

1933	Air Post	1	perf						airplanes
1936	Regular Mail	2	perf						
1989	Regular Mail	1	perf						

NETHERLANDS ANTILLES

1955	Regular Mail	1	perf						
1984	Regular Mail	3	perf						

NETHERLANDS INDIES

1933	Air Post	1	perf						airplanes

NEVIS

1987	Regular Mail	8	perf						fish

NEW HEBRIDES

The two issues of triangular stamps have the same design, but have their inscriptions in two languages, English and French. This is due to the islands having joint English and French administrations. (Note: In the Scott catalogs, these listings are split into two different volumes: one in the British Commonwealth and one in countries of the world.)

1974	Regular Mail	2	perf						
1974	Regular Mail	2	perf						

NEW ZEALAND

1943	Semi-Postal	2	perf						
1995	Semi-Postal	2	perf						

Souvenir sheets were also issued.

1997	Regular Mail	2	perf						birds

A souvenir sheet was also issued.

NEWFOUNDLAND

These two issues differ in only the paper and mesh used.

1857	Regular Mail	1	imperf						
1860	Regular Mail	1	imperf						

NICARAGUA

1947	Regular Mail	11	perf						
1947	Air Post	13	perf						
1947	Air Post Official	8	perf						10,000 sets
1956	Regular Mail	1/6	perf						
1971	Air Post	1/14	perf						

Year	Type of Mail Service	Catalog No.	No. in set	Separation Type	Check-off boxes				Topic
					Mint	CTO	Used	Cover	

NIGERIA

1963	Regular Mail		2	perf					scouting

There is also a souvenir sheet.

1964	Regular Mail		1/4	perf					sports

There is also a souvenir sheet.

NYASSA

1924	Postage Due		9	perf					animals

OBOCK

1893	Regular Mail		2	imperf					
1894	Regular Mail		5	imperf					

PAKISTAN

1961	Regular Mail		2	perf					
1962	Regular Mail		1	perf					
1985	Regular Mail		1	perf					scouting

PANAMA

Note: Where these Panama sets have imperforates, they are of the same design but in different colors than the perforated items.

1964	Regular Mail		6	perf					space

Souvenir sheets were also issued.

1964	Regular Mail		6	imperf					space
1964	Regular Mail		6	perf					space

Souvenir sheets were also issued.

1965	Regular Mail		8	imperf					Kennedy
1965	Regular Mail		8	perf					Kennedy

Souvenir sheets were also issued.

1965	Regular Mail		6	imperf					nuclear
1965	Regular Mail		6	perf					nuclear

Souvenir sheets were also issued.

1965	Air Post		2	imperf					Galileo
1965	Air Post		2	perf					Galileo

Souvenir sheets were also issued.

1965	Air Post		2	imperf					Nobel
1965	Air Post		2	perf					Nobel

Souvenir sheets were also issued.

Year	Type of Mail Service	Catalog No.	No. in set	Separation Type	Check-off boxes Mint	CTO	Used	Cover	Topic
1968	Regular Mail		4	both					space

Souvenir sheets were also issued.

| 1968 | Regular Mail | | 8 | both | | | | | space |

Souvenir sheets were also issued.

| 1984 | Regular Mail | | 4 | perf | | | | | sports |

There is also a souvenir sheet.

PAPUA NEW GUINEA

| 1988 | Regular Mail | | 1/2 | perf | | | | | |

PARAGUAY

1932	Regular Mail		5	perf					zeppelin; 10,000 sets
1932	Air Post		5	perf					zeppelin
1935	Air Post		4	perf					
1965	Regular Mail		8	imperf					scientists; 7,000 sets
1965	Regular Mail		8	perf					scientists

Souvenir sheets were also issued.

PERU

| 1931 | Regular Mail | | 4/7 | perf | | | | | |

PHILIPPINES

| 1960 | Regular Mail | | 1 | perf | | | | | |
| 1960 | Air Post | | 1 | perf | | | | | |

POLAND

| 1959 | Regular Mail | | 8 | perf | | | | | |
| 1963 | Regular Mail | | 3/10 | perf | | | | | |

QATAR

1965	Regular Mail		5/8	imperf					scouting
1965	Regular Mail		5/8	perf					scouting
1966	Regular Mail	m{184}	5/8	imperf					scouting
1966	Regular Mail	m{184}	5/8	perf					scouting
1992	Regular Mail		2/4	perf					

Year	Type of Mail Service	Catalog No.	No. in set	Separation Type	Check-off boxes				Topic
					Mint	CTO	Used	Cover	

ROMANIA

Year	Type of Mail Service	Catalog No.	No. in set	Separation Type	Mint	CTO	Used	Cover	Topic
1945	Air Post Semi-Post		2	imperf					airplanes
1948	Semi-Postal		1/5	imperf					

This stamp also was issued as a mini-sheet of four stamps in the shape of a large triangle.

| 1957 | Regular Mail | | 1/4 | perf | | | | | |

This stamp was produced in sheets which included 20 different triangular tabs inscribed, "Peace and Friendship," in 20 different languages.

| 1960 | Air Post | | 2/6 | perf | | | | | butterflies |
| 1965 | Regular Mail | | 1/8 | perf | | | | | dogs |

RUSSIA

Note that Russia has issued CTOs since the 1940s.

1922	Semi-Postal		1/4	imperf					
1965	Regular Mail		1	perf					
1965	Regular Mail		1	perf					
1966	Regular Mail		2/3	perf					

These two triangulars and the third item in the set, which is a diamond, were printed so that the set of 3 form a larger triangle.

| 1966 | Regular Mail | | 3 | perf | | | | | sports |

Each of the three stamps in this set has a tab attached. The tab is the upper triangle and the stamp is the lower triangle, with the pair forming a square. The two triangles are separated by perforations. This is an example of the triangle "resting" on its apex.

1966	Regular Mail		3	perf					sports
1967	Regular Mail		1	perf					
1971	Regular Mail		5	perf					automobiles
1973	Regular Mail		1	perf					
1973	Regular Mail		3	perf					
1973	Regular Mail		5	perf					animals
1976	Regular Mail		1	perf					
1981	Regular Mail		1	perf					
1984	Regular Mail		1	perf					

This Christmas/New Year's stamp is available as a mini-sheet of eight.

| 1989 | Regular Mail | | 1 | perf | | | | | |
| 1990 | Regular Mail | | 1 | perf | | | | | |

This Christmas/New Year's stamp is available as a mini-sheet of eight.

| 1993 | Regular Mail | | 1 | perf | | | | | |

This Christmas/New Year's stamp is available as a mini-sheet of eight.

Year	Type of Mail Service	Catalog No.	No. in set	Separation Type	Check-off boxes				Topic
					Mint	CTO	Used	Cover	

SALVADOR, EL

Year	Type of Mail Service	Catalog No.	No. in set	Separation Type	Mint	CTO	Used	Cover	Topic
1921	Regular Mail		1/8	perf					coins
1921	Regular Mail		1/4	perf					coins
1924	Regular Mail		1/2	perf					coins
1924	Regular Mail		1	perf					coins
1973	Regular Mail		2	perf					lions
1973	Air Post		2	perf					lions

SAN MARINO

Year	Type of Mail Service	Catalog No.	No. in set	Separation Type	Mint	CTO	Used	Cover	Topic
1952	Air Post		3/6	perf					flowers
1953	Regular Mail		2/9	perf					sports
1959	Regular Mail		1	perf					sports

SHARJAH

Year	Type of Mail Service	Catalog No.	No. in set	Separation Type	Mint	CTO	Used	Cover	Topic
1964	Regular Mail		8	imperf					Olympics
1964	Regular Mail		8	perf					Olympics

There is also a souvenir sheet.

Year	Type of Mail Service	Catalog No.	No. in set	Separation Type	Mint	CTO	Used	Cover	Topic
1965	Regular Mail		20	imperf					science
1965	Regular Mail		20	perf					science

Souvenir sheets were also issued.

Year	Type of Mail Service	Catalog No.	No. in set	Separation Type	Mint	CTO	Used	Cover	Topic
1966	Regular Mail	m{269}	20	imperf					science
1966	Regular Mail	m{269}	20	perf					science

Souvenir sheets were also issued.

Year	Type of Mail Service	Catalog No.	No. in set	Separation Type	Mint	CTO	Used	Cover	Topic
1966	Regular Mail	m{A299}	8	perf					Olympics

SOMALI COAST

Year	Type of Mail Service	Catalog No.	No. in set	Separation Type	Mint	CTO	Used	Cover	Topic
1894	Regular Mail		2	imperf					
1894	Regular Mail		1	imperf					ships

Although this is an imperf stamp it has printed "perforations" around the perimeter of the stamp, which is very unusual and attractive.

Year	Type of Mail Service	Catalog No.	No. in set	Separation Type	Mint	CTO	Used	Cover	Topic
1902	Regular Mail		5	imperf					
1943	Regular Mail		2	perf					

SOUTH AFRICA

These two differ from each other in that one has an English inscription, while the other has its inscription in Afrikaans. These came in sheets of one language or the other. Although the government issued them only as imperf sheets, some sheets were privately perforated and rouletted for the convenience of removing individual stamps.

Year	Type of Mail Service	Catalog No.	No. in set	Separation Type	Mint	CTO	Used	Cover	Topic
1926	Regular Mail		2	imperf					

SOUTH WEST AFRICA

Of these items, three are imperforate while two were perforated by a private firm. The South Africa was overprinted with "SOUTH WEST AFRICA" in three different styles of over-printing.

Year	Type of Mail Service	Catalog No.	No. in set	Separation Type	Mint	CTO	Used	Cover	Topic
1926	Regular Mail		5	imperf and perf					

SPAIN

Year	Type of Mail Service	Catalog No.	No. in set	Separation Type	Mint	CTO	Used	Cover	Topic
1930	Regular Mail		3/16	imperf					ships; 1,000 sets
1930	Regular Mail		3/16	perf					ships

These Columbus commemoratives were privately produced but valid for postage for three days, thus making them "legitimate" postage stamps.

SRI LANKA

Year	Type of Mail Service	Catalog No.	No. in set	Separation Type	Mint	CTO	Used	Cover	Topic
1982	Regular Mail		1	perf					
1996	Regular Mail		4	perf					sports

ST. VINCENT

Year	Type of Mail Service	Catalog No.	No. in set	Separation Type	Mint	CTO	Used	Cover	Topic
1973	Regular Mail		4	perf					Columbus
1975	Regular Mail		12	perf					Christmas

This set of 12 is composed of four of the 3c denomination, printed so they form a larger triangle. The other eight stamps are se-tenant pairs of four denominations with each pair being in a different color.

SURINAM

Year	Type of Mail Service	Catalog No.	No. in set	Separation Type	Mint	CTO	Used	Cover	Topic
1960	Regular Mail		5	perf					airplanes
1985	Regular Mail		12	perf					trains
1986	Regular Mail		2	perf					trains
1987	Regular Mail		12	perf					airplanes
1988	Regular Mail		2/3	perf					trains
1989	Regular Mail		12	perf					automobiles
1990	Regular Mail		12	perf					flowers
1991	Regular Mail		12	perf					snakes
1991	?		4	perf					trains
1992	Regular Mail		2	perf					trains
1993	Regular Mail		12	perf					insects
1994	Regular Mail		12	perf					butterflies
1994	Regular Mail		2	perf					transportation
1995	Regular Mail		12	perf					flowers
1996	Regular Mail		12	perf					flowers
1997	Regular Mail		12	perf					monkeys

Year	Type of Mail Service	Catalog No.	No. in set	Separation Type	Check-off boxes				Topic
					Mint	CTO	Used	Cover	

TANNU TUVA

Year	Type of Mail Service	Catalog No.	No. in set	Separation Type	Mint	CTO	Used	Cover	Topic
1933	Regular Mail		2/14	perf					
1933	Regular Mail		2	perf					

Note: For issues after 1933, there is a question as to whether they were issued by an authorized governmental agency. Some catalogers consider these latter issues to be bogus, and to be Cinderella items. The 1941 items are not commonly available. They exist in very small quantities and are expensive.

Year	Type of Mail Service	Catalog No.	No. in set	Separation Type	Mint	CTO	Used	Cover	Topic
1934	Regular Mail	m{(51)}	4/9	perf					
1935	Regular Mail	m{59}	4/7	perf					
1935	Regular Mail	m{(69)}	7/10	perf					
1936	Regular Mail	m{(79)}	8/22	perf					
1936	Air Post	m{98}	3/9	perf					
1941	Regular Mail	m{(117)}	1/8	perf					
1941	Regular Mail	m{(124)}	3/5	perf					

UNITED STATES of AMERICA

Year	Type of Mail Service	Catalog No.	No. in set	Separation Type	Mint	CTO	Used	Cover	Topic
1997	Regular Mail		2	perf					transportation

There are also four triangular tabs with this issue.

URUGUAY

Year	Type of Mail Service	Catalog No.	No. in set	Separation Type	Mint	CTO	Used	Cover	Topic
1929	Parcel Post		7	perf					2,945 sets
1933	Regular Mail		6	perf					birds
1934	Air Post		2	perf					birds; 8,236 sets

These 1933 and 1934 issues were issued only in mini-sheets of six stamps of the same denomination.

Year	Type of Mail Service	Catalog No.	No. in set	Separation Type	Mint	CTO	Used	Cover	Topic
1943	Parcel Post		7	perf					2,750 sets

VENEZUELA

Year	Type of Mail Service	Catalog No.	No. in set	Separation Type	Mint	CTO	Used	Cover	Topic
1973	Regular Mail		7	perf					

VIETNAM

Year	Type of Mail Service	Catalog No.	No. in set	Separation Type	Mint	CTO	Used	Cover	Topic
1970	Regular Mail		4	perf					birds

YEMEN-PEOPLES D R

Year	Type of Mail Service	Catalog No.	No. in set	Separation Type	Mint	CTO	Used	Cover	Topic
1970	Regular Mail		4	perf					animals
1981	Regular Mail		3	perf					animals

YEMEN-MUTAWAKELITE KINGDOM

Year	Type of Mail Service	Catalog No.	No. in set	Separation Type	Mint	CTO	Used	Cover	Topic
1965	Regular Mail	m{188}	3	imperf					9,100 sets
1965	Regular Mail	m{188}	3	perf					

There is also a souvenir sheet.

Year	Type of Mail Service	Catalog No.	No. in set	Separation Type	Mint	CTO	Used	Cover	Topic

Diagonal perforated bisects

GUATEMALA

Year	Type of Mail Service	Catalog No.	No. in set	Separation Type	Mint	CTO	Used	Cover	Topic
1935	Regular Mail		1	perf					Lake scene
1941	Regular Mail		1	perf					Portrait
1951	Air Post		1	perf					Mission

LOURENCO MARQUES

Year	Type of Mail Service	Catalog No.	No. in set	Separation Type	Mint	CTO	Used	Cover	Topic
1915	Regular Mail		1	perf					
1915	Regular Mail		1	perf					

PARAGUAY

Year	Type of Mail Service	Catalog No.	No. in set	Separation Type	Mint	CTO	Used	Cover	Topic
1911	Regular Mail		1	perf					

PORTUGESE INDIA

Year	Type of Mail Service	Catalog No.	No. in set	Separation Type	Mint	CTO	Used	Cover	Topic
1911	Regular Mail		1	perf					

Postal stationery

Year	Type of Mail Service	Catalog No.	No. of Items	Separation Type	Mint	Used	Cover	Topic

MOZAMBIQUE

Year	Type of Mail Service	Catalog No.	No. of Items	Separation Type	Mint	Used	Cover	Topic
1961	Regular Mail		1	-				

SWITZERLAND

These three items all have the same printed postage. However, there are other printed differences between them. One has a printed pattern of small white symbols on the blue-gray paper. The two without the patterned paper have their return address section printed either upright or upside-down.

Year	Type of Mail Service	Catalog No.	No. of Items	Separation Type	Mint	Used	Cover	Topic
1963	Regular Mail		3	-				

UNITED STATES

Year	Type of Mail Service	Catalog No.	No. of Items	Separation Type	Mint	Used	Cover	Topic
1956	Post Card		1	-				
1965	Stamped Envelope		1	-				
1968	Stamped Envelope		1	-				
1968	Stamped Envelope		1	-				

The 1965 Stamped Envelope had an added surcharge of 2 cents to bring it to the new air mail postage rate.

Year	Type of Mail Service	Catalog No.	No. of Items	Separation Type	Mint	Used	Cover	Topic
1971	Stamped Envelope		1	-				

The 1968 Stamped Envelope had an added surcharge of 1 cent to bring it to the new air mail postage rate.

Year	Type of Mail Service	Catalog No.	No. of Items	Separation Type	Check-off boxes			Topic
					Mint	Used	Cover	

Souvenir sheets

Note: The number of stamps column indicates the total number of stamps contained on all the sheets in the set.

BANGLADESH

Year	Type of Mail Service	Catalog No.	No. of Items	Separation Type	Mint	Used	Cover	Topic
1984	Regular Mail	1	2	perf				stamp

COOK ISLANDS

This souvenir sheet of 12 items has 10 different stamps, with two of each denomination printed se-tenant, and two labels.

Year	Type of Mail Service	Catalog No.	No. of Items	Separation Type	Mint	Used	Cover	Topic
1969	Regular Mail	1	10	perf				sports

COSTA RICA

Year	Type of Mail Service	Catalog No.	No. of Items	Separation Type	Mint	Used	Cover	Topic
1937	Regular Mail	1	4	imperf				

HAITI

These souvenir sheets are imperforate. One sheet has an inscription line, "Contribution d'Haiti à 1'OMS," while the other sheet does not.

Year	Type of Mail Service	Catalog No.	No. of Items	Separation Type	Mint	Used	Cover	Topic
1962	Air Post	2	6	imperf				

HUNGARY

Year	Type of Mail Service	Catalog No.	No. of Items	Separation Type	Mint	Used	Cover	Topic
1958	Regular Mail	1	4	imperf				flowers
1958	Regular Mail	1	4	perf				flowers

IRAQ

Year	Type of Mail Service	Catalog No.	No. of Items	Separation Type	Mint	Used	Cover	Topic
1965	Regular Mail	1	1	imperf				

ISRAEL

This souvenir sheet was issued for Israel's First International Stamp Exhibition. Although it appears as a solid sheet, closer examination reveals there are four roulette cut triangles in the center of the sheet.

Year	Type of Mail Service	Catalog No.	No. of Items	Separation Type	Mint	Used	Cover	Topic
1957	Regular Mail	1	4	roulette				philately

JORDAN

Year	Type of Mail Service	Catalog No.	No. of Items	Separation Type	Mint	Used	Cover	Topic
1964	Regular Mail	1	1	imperf				Kennedy
1964	Regular Mail	1	1	imperf				Olympics
1964	Regular Mail	1	1	imperf				scouting

Year	Type of Mail Service	Catalog No.	No. of Items	Separation Type	Mint	Used	Cover	Topic

KENYA

Year	Type of Mail Service	Catalog No.	No. of Items	Separation Type	Mint	Used	Cover	Topic
1982	Regular Mail	1	1	perf				sports
1987	Regular Mail	1	1	perf				

LIBYA

Year	Type of Mail Service	Catalog No.	No. of Items	Separation Type	Mint	Used	Cover	Topic
1962	Regular Mail	1	3	imperf				

MALDIVE ISLANDS

Year	Type of Mail Service	Catalog No.	No. of Items	Separation Type	Mint	Used	Cover	Topic
1968	Regular Mail	1	2	imperf				space
1975	Regular Mail	1	1	imperf				sea

MARSHALL ISLANDS

These two sheets each have two stamps and five triangular tabs.

Year	Type of Mail Service	Catalog No.	No. of Items	Separation Type	Mint	Used	Cover	Topic
1997	Regular Mail	2	4	perf				ships

NEW ZEALAND

Year	Type of Mail Service	Catalog No.	No. of Items	Separation Type	Mint	Used	Cover	Topic
1995	Regular Mail	2	8	perf				

One sheet has "Issued in Support of Stampex '95" printed on it, while the other does not.

Year	Type of Mail Service	Catalog No.	No. of Items	Separation Type	Mint	Used	Cover	Topic
1997	Regular Mail	1	4	perf				

NICARAGUA

This sheet contains one stamp oriented so that its base is not its longest side.

Year	Type of Mail Service	Catalog No.	No. of Items	Separation Type	Mint	Used	Cover	Topic
1982	Air Post	1	1	perf				balloon

NIGERIA

Year	Type of Mail Service	Catalog No.	No. of Items	Separation Type	Mint	Used	Cover	Topic
1963	Regular Mail	1	2	perf				scouts
1964	Regular Mail	1	4	imperf				sports

This sheet appears to have four perforated stamps in a solid colored background. However, the perforations are only printed and the sheet is really an imperf item. The four stamps are all the same item.

PANAMA

Year	Type of Mail Service	Catalog No.	No. of Items	Separation Type	Mint	Used	Cover	Topic
1964	Regular Mail	1	1	imperf				space
1964	Regular Mail	1	1	perf				space
1964	Regular Mail	1	1	imperf				space
1964	Regular Mail	1	1	perf				space
1965	Regular Mail	1	1	imperf				Kennedy
1965	Regular Mail	1	1	perf				Kennedy
1965	Regular Mail	1	2	imperf				nuclear
1965	Regular Mail	1	2	perf				nuclear

Year	Type of Mail Service	Catalog No.	No. of Items	Separation Type	Check-off boxes Mint	Used	Cover	Topic
1965	Air Post	2	2	imperf				Galileo
1965	Air Post	2	2	perf				Galileo
1965	Air Post	1	2	imperf				Nobel
1965	Air Post	1	2	perf				Nobel
1968	Regular Mail	2	2	both				space
1968	Regular Mail	3	3	perf				space
1984	Regular Mail	1	1	perf				Olympics

PARAGUAY

Year	Type of Mail Service	Catalog No.	No. of Items	Separation Type	Mint	Used	Cover	Topic
1965	Regular Mail	1	2	imperf				scientists; 6,000 issued
1965	Regular Mail	1	2	perf				scientists; 6,000 issued
1974	Air Post	1	1	imperf				balloons; 4,000 issued

ROMANIA

Year	Type of Mail Service	Catalog No.	No. of Items	Separation Type	Mint	Used	Cover	Topic
1945	Regular Mail	1	1	perf				aircraft
1945	Regular Mail	1	1	imperf				aircraft

SHARJAH

Year	Type of Mail Service	Catalog No.	No. of Items	Separation Type	Mint	Used	Cover	Topic
1964	Regular Mail	1	1	imperf				Olympics
1965	Regular Mail	2	4	imperf				science
1966	Regular Mail	m{289}	2	imperf				science

SRI LANKA

Year	Type of Mail Service	Catalog No.	No. of Items	Separation Type	Mint	Used	Cover	Topic
1996	Regular Mail	1	4	perf				sports

SPAIN

Year	Type of Mail Service	Catalog No.	No. of Items	Separation Type	Mint	Used	Cover	Topic
1992	Regular Mail	1	1	perf				ships
1992	Semi-Postal	1	3	perf				ships

This sheet has reproductions of the "classic" three Columbus triangles from the 1930 issue, only the denominations in the two lower corners has changed. The sheet also has a triangular tab.

ST. VINCENT

The stamps in this issue were only issued as a souvenir sheet. This is the second set of self-adhesive triangulars ever issued.

Year	Type of Mail Service	Catalog No.	No. of Items	Separation Type	Mint	Used	Cover	Topic
1996	Regular Mail	1	3	perf				movies

YEMEN-MUTAWAKELITE KINGDOM

Year	Type of Mail Service	Catalog No.	No. of Items	Separation Type	Mint	Used	Topic
1965	Regular Mail	m{188} 1	3	imperf			10,000 issued

Year	Type of Mail Service	Catalog No.	No. in set	Separation Type	Check-off boxes				Topic
					Mint	CTO	Used	Cover	

Triangular-stamps-on-stamps

ANGUILLA

| 1979 | Regular Mail | | 1/6 | perf | | | | | |

There is also a souvenir sheet which contains the stamp.

| 1990 | Regular Mail | | 1/4 | perf | | | | | |

There is also a souvenir sheet which contains the stamp.

COSTA RICA

| 1975 | Air Post | | 4 | perf | | | | | |
| 1982 | Air Post | | 8 | perf | | | | | |

DJIBOUTI

| 1987 | Souvenir sheet | | 1 | perf | | | | | |

FALKLAND ISLANDS

| 1991 | Regular Mail | | 4 | perf | | | | | |

FAEROE ISLANDS

| 1979 | Regular Mail | | 2 | perf | | | | | |

GUERNSEY

| 1990 | Regular Mail | | 1 | perf | | | | | |

There is also a souvenir sheet which contains the stamp.

MONTSERRAT

| 1976 | Regular Mail | | 1 | perf | | | | | |

PARAGUAY

1968	Regular Mail		1/9	perf					zeppelin
1968	Souvenir sheet		1	perf					zeppelin, 4,000 issued
1971	Regular Mail	m{2198}	1	perf					zeppelin; 4,000 issued

SOUTH AFRICA

| 1953 | Regular Mail | | 2 | perf | | | | | |

UGANDA

Although the stamp is not a triangular and does not depict a triangular, the souvenir sheet does depict a triangular stamp, namely, a Rattlesnake Island local post Cinderella.

| 1994 | Souvenir sheet | | 1 | perf | | | | | airplane |

Chapter 10

Revenue Listing

One of the main purposes for these listings is to permit others to identify triangular items. The listings provide descriptive material and inscriptions, the words printed on the stamp, for establishing a positive identification of a particular item. An illustration is preferable, but with publishing and item availability constraints it was possible to provide illustrations for only a fraction of the items.

Some notes regarding the information presented for each of the items:

- The "country" associated with an issue is indicated for only the first set for that country. Items are listed from the oldest to the newest set when there is more than one set of items for a country.
- The "number in set" is the total number of different labels or seals created. Changes in design, color or separation all create a different item. When there is no reference work for the items this number may be incomplete—since without a reference, the number is based on items personally seen in various collections.
- The "item number" is the number this author assigned the item or set of items. Since so many of the Cinderellas do not have an identification number given in some other reference work, it is appropriate for this handbook to provide a shorthand reference. For uniformity, item numbers have also been assigned where other catalogers' numbers already exist. In those cases, the other identification number is provided in the accompanying text. When this handbook includes an illustration of the item, the key word "photo" appears with the item number.
- Author's comments that are not part of the documentation are enclosed within ( ). Often these request more information.
- The reference notation uses the following model:
  (REF) indicates a reference notation; # precedes a reference number (the number is the identification number of the reference found in the bibliography at the back of this handbook); / precedes either a page number or a specific issue designation; specific volumes are indicated by "vol," which may be followed by an issue number; a semi-colon is used to indicate the end of a reference when there is more than one reference source for an item.

This presentation style applies to both the revenue and Cinderella listings.

Revenues are stamps used to indicate a duty or tax paid to the issuing authority in the amount of the stamp and for the purpose stated on the stamp. These are also called "fiscals."

Country	Year	Item		Mint	Used	Cover
	No. in set	Separation	Item Number			
Description						

AZORES   1894-1901–Contribuicao Industrial
216   imperf   R020

These items are overprints of the revenues issued by Portugal–overprinted with "ACORES." See the Portugal section below for details (REF#189/57).

R040   R040   R060   R040

COLOMBIA   1889-1908–Habilitacion (Republique)
52   imperf   R040 (photo)

These revenue items use various design motifs, but they have commonality in their border areas. One side contains the word "HABILITACION," another has "BIENIO" and the years, and the third side has the denomination. Items 1-21 are on white paper. Items 22-47 are with black printing. The 1905 surcharge, done on the 1903-1904 issues, reads "Habilitacion 1905 A. Ruiz Z."

Forbin No.	Years	Denom.	Printing color
1	1889-1890	20c	brown
2	1889-1890	50c	blue
3	1889-1890	1p	red
4	1891-1892	20c	black
5	1891-1892	50c	blue
6	1891-1892	1p	vermilion
7	1893-1894	20c	black
8	1893-1894	50c	ultramarine
9	1893-1894	1p	red
10	1895-1896	20c	black
11	1895-1896	50c	blue
12	1895-1896	1p	red
13	1897-1898	20c	black
	1897-1898	30c	black
14	1897-1898	50c	blue
15	1897-1898	1p	red
16	1897-1898	30c	black
17	1897-1898	1p	blue
18	1897-1898	2p	red
19	1899-1900	20c	black
20	1899-1900	1p	blue
21	1899-1900	2p	red

Forbin No.	Years	Denom.	Paper color	Surcharge color
22	1901-1902	30c	yellow	
23	1901-1902	60c	salmon	
24	1901-1902	1p	blue	
25	1901-1902	2p	pink	
26	1903-1904	30c	pink	
27	1903-1904	70c	pink	
28	1903-1904	1p	teal	
29	1903-1904	2p	blue	
30	1903-1904	2.4p	green	
31	1903-1904	3p	yellow	
32	1903-1904	3p	salmon	
33	1903-1904	3p	blue	
34	1903-1904	4.8p	blue	
35	1903-1904	10p	blue	
36	1905	3p	salmon	black
37	1905	2p	blue	violet
38	1905	3p	salmon	violet
39	1905	4.8p	green	violet
40	1905-1906	2p	blue	
41	1905-1906	3p	blue	
42	1905-1906	10p	green	
43	1905-1906	15p	pink	
44	1906-1908	10c	rose	
45	1906-1908	2p	?	
46	1906-1908	5p	?	
47	1906-1908	10p	?	

Morley indicates some additional items: 1889–50c black on orange; 1891–30c black on yellow. Morley also illustrates a different design than appears in Forbin (REF#1500/259; #3930/113).

I also have a 1903-1904 10p in black on green; 1903-1904 15p in black on pink. (Do you have any others in your collection?)

1901-1902–Habilitacion (Medellin)
8   imperf   R060 (photo)

The city of Medellin issued these revenues. They differ from the other Colombian triangular revenues in appearance–they do *not* have an even border, nor a truly central design. They do have multiple horizontal lines of inscriptions. Compare photos R040 with R060. For items #1 and #2, a class is indicated on the stamp–that is, the stamp is inscribed with "CLASE"; for items #3 through #6, there is no class indication. They are all on white paper (REF#1500/261).

Forbin No.	Years	Denom.	Printing color
1	1901-1902	30c	black
2	1901-1902	1p	blue
3	1901-1902	30c	black
4	1901-1902	30c	yellow
5	1901-1902	1p	blue
6	1901-1902	2p	red

I also have a 1901-1902 2p in black on white paper and on pink paper.

1901-1904–Habilitacion (Carthagene)
5   imperf   R080

The city of Carthagene issued these revenues. In appearance they are like the ones for the Republique. They use various design motifs, but they have commonality in their border areas. One side contains the word "HABILITACION," another has "BIENIO" and the years, and the third side has the denomination (REF#1500/260).

Forbin No.	Years	Denom.	Printing color
2	1901-1902	30c	blue on white paper
3	1901-1902	60c	black on yellow paper
4	1901-1902	1p	black on blue paper
5	1901-1902	3p	black on white paper
6	1903-1904	3p	black on white paper

CZECHOSLOVAKIA 192?–Gorkau municipal issue
1   perf   R100

This is a municipal issue from Gorkau, a city due North of Pilsen near the border. The denomination of 1Kc is printed at the apex of the triangle, which is oriented with the apex downward. The city's name appears on the first of four lines of black printing on the gray paper (REF#1839/122).

JERSEY   1915–Property guarantee fund
7   perf   R120

There are five denominations and designs: 1/- carmine of a cow, 2/- green of a building, 5/- vermilion of arms, 10/- blue of a harbor, and 1£ brown of a battle scene. Each of the two low values was issued in two different perfs, 12 and 14 . The 1£ is inscribed "Etates de Jersey Une Livre Sterling" (REF#340/13).

R140   R160   R180   R180

PANAMA   1917-1918– documentary fees(?)
11   perf   R140 (photo)

There are two kinds that I have seen. One is a "1 PARTE DECLARACION" stamp, which comes in (at least) 10 values ranging from 1 centesimo to 10 balboas, with each denomination having its own color. The other is a "2 PARTE ENCOMIENDA" stamp possibly in the same colors and denominations as the other type. The inscriptions include, "REPUBLICA DE PANAMA SECRETARIA DE HACIENDA Y TESORO DERECHOS SOBRE ENCOMIENDAS," which refers to the "secretary of finance and treasury" and to a "tax (or commission) on land holdings."

The design is of half of Panama's coat of arms. (See Panama's 1909 2-1/2c item which depicts a full coat of arms.)

PORTUGAL   1894-1901–Contribuicao Industrial
216   imperf   R160 (photo)

In each year, there were 27 denominations issued ranging from 2 reis to 20,000 reis. The design for all the stamps is a coat of arms with a crown on top inscribed on two sides with, "CONTRIBUICAO INDUSTRIAL." The year and denomination are overprinted on the stamp. The stamps for 1894-1899 are of five colors with the same color used for the same denomination in each year. Then, in 1900, the colors changed and remained in effect for 1901 (REF#189/20; #1500/640).

RUSSIA   **1926–Fee for Radiodiffusion**
        10   perf   R180 (photo)
    The central design is an old-fashioned radio vacuum tube. The denominations are in the two lower corners. There is an inscription in all three borders. These 10 items come in two sizes–the smaller is for denominations of 1, 2, 3, 4, 10, and 50 kopecks, with the larger size being 1, 3, 5, and 10 rubles (REF#5375/92).

Denomination	Size	Border color	Center color
1 K	small	yellow	yellow
2 K	small	mauve	mauve
3 K	small	green	green
5 K	small	blue	blue
10 K	small	pink	pink
50 K	small	brown	green
1 R	larger	red	yellow
3 R	larger	orange	green
5 R	larger	red	blue
10R	larger	gray	red

R200   R220

SPAIN   **1937–Overtax-Tafalla**
        8   perf and imperf   R200 (photo)
    In August 1936, the Spanish government authorized cities to collect, if they wanted to, an extra 5 centimos on any mailing done in the city. This revenue was to create and operate places for feeding people hurt by the Civil War.
    Tafalla was one of only two cities that used the triangular format for these "overtax" stamps. All eight items are inscribed, "TAFALLA BENE~FICENCIA," and depict an obelisk with a coat of arms,on the left and the denomination on the right. Four of the items are 5cts denomination–a forest green and an apple green in perf and imperf forms. The four 10cts items are a purple-carmine and a dark blue both in perf and imperf forms (REF#1726/382).

        1938–Overtax-Nerja
        2   imperf   R220 (photo)
    Nerja is the other city issuing a triangular Civil War overtax stamp. There are two items– a green and red 5 cts stamp, and the same design in a souvenir sheet. The vignette is of an airplane flying over a large ancient bridge or aqueduct(?) between two hills and inscribed, "8-2-1937 1st ANIVERSARIO 8-2-1938 PRO-NERJA." The souvenir sheet contains only one stamp (REF#1726/367).

Chapter 11

Cinderella Listing

Labels and seals–charity fund-raising

Adhesive labels and seals exist for many purposes. Often, they were used on letters in addition to postage stamps. The sender used them to let others know of an event, business or charity they support.

ARGENTINA 1949-1955–Leprosy seals
7 perf LS1020 (photo)

Each year, from 1949-1955, a charity label, like a Christmas seal, was issued to raise money for the fight against leprosy. These items all depict a ringing bell and are inscribed with, "PATRONATO DE LEPROSOS DE LA REPUBLICA ARGENTINA." They are all on white paper.

Year	Denomination	Colors
1949-50	10 cents	yellow and green
1951	10 cents	yellow and deeper green
1952	10 cents	aqua and brown
1953	10 cents	light green and brown
1954	$1	orange and brown
1955	$1	yellow and brown
1955	$3.60	forest green and brown

Whether the triangular form was used before 1949 and after 1955 I do not know–maybe I will be able to find out for the 2nd edition of this handbook.

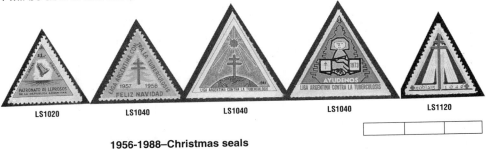

LS1020   LS1040   LS1040   LS1040   LS1120

1956-1988–Christmas seals
77 rouletted LS1040 (photo)

The Argentine League Against Tuberculosis issued triangular-shaped stamps to raise money for TB aid. Each year's issue has a distinctive design that includes the year and the agency's name, "Liga Argentina Contra la Tuberculosis." Exceptions to the normal issuance characteristics are as follows:

- Stamps from 1956-1961 are perforated.
- The 1956-57 issue comes in two color schemes–one with dark blue border and the other with a light blue border.
- The 1958 and 1959 issues were not triangles.

- The 1969 issue has two different designs.
- The 1979 issue has 10 different designs.
- The 1981 issue had three different designs.
- The 1982 issue had four different designs.
- The 1983 issue had eight different designs.

The last year in the references I used was 1988. Did they cease issuing stamps, did they change from issuing triangles, or were more triangles issued? (REF#1875; #8320/May 82/March 85/Feb. 86/April 87)

1958–Red Cross seal
1   imperf   **LS1060**

This issue has a large bold red cross with 1 Peso denomination surrounded by a border inscription, "CRUZ ROJA ARGENTINA COMITE PRO-MONUMENTO A LA MADRE (1958)," in blue and black (REF#2566/2).

AUSTRALIA   **1978–Christmas seal**
1   roulette   **LS1080**

This seal has a purple background illustrated with a pair of hands and "hope" in white, an outline of a person in a wheelchair and a TB symbol in red. The label is inscribed with "Bedford Industries Christmas 1978."

1980–Christmas seal
1   roulette   **LS1100**

A carmine background illustrated with a pair of very stylized outstretched hands, an outline of a person in a wheelchair and a symbol in white and gold printing. The label is inscribed with, "BEDFORD INDUSTRIES 1980 CHRISTMAS."

IRELAND   **1946–Red Cross seals**
2   perf   **LS1120 (photo)**

The design is of a large red double cross—the tuberculosis symbol—with a red inscription at the bottom "noblais 1946." One version has blue and yellow in the background, while the other has blue and orange (REF#2566/162).

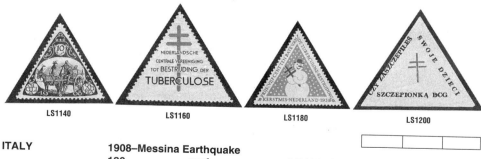

LS1140   LS1160   LS1180   LS1200

ITALY   **1908–Messina Earthquake**
120   perf   **LS1140 (photo)**

Issued to raise funds for the relief of children orphaned by the catastrophic earthquake that destroyed the city of Messina on the Isle of Sicily on Dec. 28, 1908. The quake killed more than 100,000 people.

Country	Year	Item		Mint	Used	Cover
	No. in set	Separation	Item Number			

Description

Sets of 11 stamps were made for sale in many different countries. The sets all have the same designs, but the denominations differ from country to country. One of each set is a larger stamp of higher denomination, printed in red, showing portraits of the King and Queen of Italy. The rest of the set's vignettes are of Italian scenes with each design printed in a different color. These were produced in sheets where a strip from the sheet contains all 10 of the designs. This means each sheet was printed in 10 different colors. Whole sheets were all of the same denomination.

To make it even more interesting, Germany issued two completely different sets. One set is just like those issued by all the other countries. But the second set is quite different:

- The stamps are all of the larger size used in the high value items.
- The designs are the same as the normal set.
- A strip of 10 has the designs in a different order than a strip of the smaller stamps.
- Each stamp is printed in two colors.
- The colors are different from the 10 colors used in the basic sets.

These items were priced the same as the basic items.

The countries and the denominations are as follows:

Country	Basic stamp	High value stamp
Austria	10 Heller	20 Heller
Denmark	10 ORE	20 ORE
France	10 C	25 C
Germany	10 PF	20 PF
Germany (lg. sz.)	10 PF	20 PF
Great Britain	1 1/2 d	2 1/2 d
Hungary	10 Filler	20 Filler
Italy	20 C	unknown if exists
Netherlands	5 ct	10 ct
Russia	5 kop	10 kop
United States	5 cents	10 cents

The Italy issue was sold on the island of Sicily. There is no reference to an alternatively priced item, and it is not clear if there were one or 10 or 11 designs of one or two denominations (REF#7375; #8500).

NETHERLANDS 1947–Tuberculosis seal
1   perf   LS1160 (photo)

This large seal has the tuberculosis double cross in red on a white background. There are four horizontal rows of inscription, "NEDERLANDSCHE CENTRALE VEREENIGING TOT BESTRIJDING DER TUBERCULOSE," in black (REF#1875/274).

1958–Christmas seals
1   perf   LS1180 (photo)

This seal shows a white snowman holding the double cross in red on a gray background with white snowflakes. The border inscription in red is, "PRIJS:VIJF CENT TEN BATE VAN DE TUBERCULOSE-BESTRIJDING KERSTMIS-NEDERLAND-1958," (REF#1875/275).

POLAND 193?–Bialystok -TB seal
2   imperf   LS1200 (photo)

Issued pre-1960s, these two items are ungummed "white" paper with a red TB cross and black lettering. The inscriptions are different on each item. One has "CZY ZASZCZEPILES SWOJE DZIECI SZCZEPIONKA BCG" and the other "ZAPISZ SIE NA CZLONKA KOMITETU DO WALKI Z GRUZLICA" (REF#1875/318).

PORTUGAL   **1950?–Animal Protection Society**
                 1   ?   **LS1220**

Issued by the SPA, Portugal's Animal Protection Society, the item depicts a horse, dog and chicken in the three corners. It is inscribed "Os animals sofrem como nos Tende piedade d'eles," which translates to "For what reason do we cause the animals to suffer? Have compassion for them." Black printing on orange paper.

RUSSIA   **1927–Moscow and Simferopol, Ukraine–TB Seals**
         2   imperf   **LS1240**

The design, on a light green background, is of a black hammer and sickle intertwined with a big red flower with dark green leaves. The apex is on top. Although the design is the same for these two items, they probably have different inscriptions, printed in black. (REF#1875/336, 338)

       1915–Kharkov, Ukraine–TB seals
         2   imperf   **LS1260**

These two items show a white daisy with yellow center and green leaves. The design has the apex at the bottom. One is on white paper and the other on violet paper (REF#1875/335).

LS1280   LS1300   LS1320   LS1340

SOUTH AFRICA   **19?–Somerset Hospital Christmas**
         1   perf   **LS1280 (photo)**

The vignette is of a nurse wearing a cape out-of-doors in winter. The border contains "CAPE OF GOOD HOPE SOMERSET HOSPITAL CHRISTMAS GREETINGS." It is printed in blue. (Other colors?)

SPAIN   **1938–postal surtax**
         4   perf and imperf   **LS1300 (photo)**

According to Galvez, these are among a large group of postage stamps that could include amounts for donation to charity. The postage was either 5 or 10 centimos, with the rest of the purchase price being voluntary and going to charity. The denominations of these stamps were up to 2 pesos. However, unlike most semi-postal stamps, there was not a requirement to use the higher value; thus, there was not a tax. It was a donation when purchasing and using stamps of higher value than the mailing rate.

Country	Year	Item		Mint	Used	Cover
	No. in set	Separation	Item Number			
Description						

The only triangulars in this large grouping are these four 5-centimos items, printed in blue or brown, either perforate or imperforate. The imperforates are quite rare. The design depicts two children's faces looking up at a statue of the Virgin Mary holding Jesus. She is surrounded by an enormous halo and on top of a conical form. They are inscribed, "Huerfanos del Cuerpo de ESTADO ESPANOL CORREOS" (REF#1726/299; #5775).

SWITZERLAND   **1939–Christmas seal**
1   perf   LS1320 (photo)

This seal has the double cross in red on a white background with a yellow border inscribed, "DISPENSAIRE ANTITUBERCULEUX DE GENEVE." The vignette includes "1939 DEUX SOUS" (REF#1875/368).

UNKNOWN   **?–Eastern Europe(?)**
1   imperf   LS1340 (photo)

The vignette has a big red cross in center, with a black "100" underneath. The background is black lines radiating outward from the "100." It is printed on white paper.

USA   **1878–Orthodox Jewish Fair**
4   perf   LS1360

Design is a profile of Moses Montefiore inscribed with "ORTHODOX JEWISH FAIR," the denomination, and "5639" (the date). These were issued as 5-cent orange brown (other reference has it as red), 10-cent ultramarine, 25-cent lilac, 50-cent green. (Note: REF#1930 has these items indicated as being imperf. REF#4058 has a picture of one that shows perforations. Thus, they either came both ways, in which case there are eight of them, or the one reference is in error. Does anyone have an imperf copy? (REF#1930; #4058/section V pg. 54)

1908–American Red Cross for Messina Earthquake
1   perf   LS1380 (photo)

At the time of the devastating earthquake in Messina, Italy, the Massachusetts branch of the American Red Cross issued this stamp and sold them at 10 cents each to raise relief funds. The design is a red cross above an erupting green-colored volcano. The border inscription in black reads, "AMERICAN NATIONAL RED CROSS RELIEF FUND ITALIAN EARTHQUAKE" (REF#2566/282).

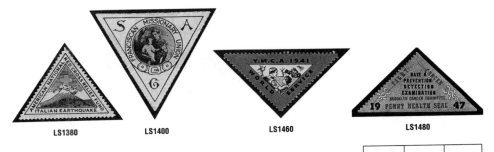

LS1380   LS1400   LS1460   LS1480

1925–Franciscan Missionary Union, Cincinnati
1   rouletted   LS1400 (photo)

This Catholic Seal, issued in Cincinnati, depicts a circular belt inscribed with "FRAN-CISCAN MISSIONARY UNION" surrounding St. Anthony holding a child. It uses dark brown printing on beige paper (REF#4058/section III pg. 10).

Pre-1930–West Side YMCA open house
1   perf   LS1420

This red and green item is inscribed "West Side YMCA New Year's Day Open House for Men" (REF#1930).

194?–Rochester YMCA member seal
1   imperf   LS1440

This red and blue on silver item is inscribed, "MEMBER ROCHESTER YMCA," with a center design of the "SPIRIT-MIND-BODY" logo (REF#4058/section VI pg. 38).

1941–YMCA World Service
1   rouletted   LS1460 (photo)

The vignette depicts a YMCA worker and child looking at a burned home. It is inscribed, "YMCA 1941 WORLD SERVICE," in black lettering on a red border (REF#4058/section VI pg. 38).

1947–Cancer Health Seal, Brooklyn
1   label has two perf and
            one rouletted side   LS1480 (photo)

This item is of a pink background with red lettering, "FIGHT CANCER PENNY HEALTH SEAL Brooklyn Cancer Committee," and in blue, "1947 Have a prevention-detection examination."

1952-1958–Children's Aid Christmas Seals
Many   rouletted   LS1500 (photo)

Various state societies for aiding children issued similarly designed Christmas seals during 1952-1958. The design is a large Christmas stocking in front of a decorated Christmas tree with "GREETINGS" inscribed below. These were issued in Kansas, Maryland, Minnesota, Washington and other states in strips of 20. Colors include red, green and blue backgrounds, with gold, silver, red or white printing.

There was also a variation produced with the stocking surrounded by a circle inscribed with the name of the issuing society (REF#4058/section X pg. 12).

LS1500

LS2060

LS4040

Country	Year	Item		Mint	Used	Cover
	No. in set	Separation	Item Number			
Description						

Labels and seals–etiquettes-airmail

FRANCE 1935–Airmail
1 imperf LS2020

A simple solid red-rose-colored triangle with the inscription "PAR AVION" in white (REF#4075/121).

SPAIN 1924, 1929–Airmail
3 imperf LS2040

These are three simple triangles as follows:

Year	Inscription	Colors	Colored border?
1924	POR AVION	red on yellow	no
1929	POR AVION	red on yellow	yes
1929	VIA AÉREA	red on yellow	yes

(REF#4075/89)

USA 1928–National Parks Airways
1 imperf LS2060 (photo)

This label depicts an Indian standing on a bluff with a Piper Cub plane flying over wild country. It is inscribed, "VIA AIR MAIL NATIONAL PARKS AIRWAYS, INC. UTAH IDAHO MONTANA."

Labels and seals–etiquettes-COD

COD labels–Collect on Delivery–are used when a sender wants to have the postal service collect from the party receiving a parcel a specified sum of money in payment for the parcel. This means the postal service needs to be sure a parcel is clearly marked as being a COD item. Several countries used brightly colored triangulars for this purpose.

LS3020   LS3020   LS3020

GERMANY 1940s–COD label
1 imperf LS3020 (photo)

A bright red-brown, or maybe orange, solid triangle with black inscription "Nr._____ Nachnahme Remboursement"

LATVIA 1937–COD parcel label
2 imperf LS3020

The two items were each simple orange triangulars inscribed, "Pëcmaksa Remboursement." There was a larger one used on the parcel itself, and a smaller one used on the accompanying documents (REF#2700/7-5).

Country	Year	Item		Mint	Used	Cover
Description	No. in set	Separation	Item Number			

SWEDEN 1907-1920–COD parcel label

6 perf and imperf LS3020 (photo)

The postal service used six different COD labels from 1907 to 1920. These labels were brightly colored and triangular in shape to catch the eye of the postal workers so they were sure to realize that money was due upon delivery.

All of the labels are a solid orange with black text. The text changed slightly over the period as indicated below:

1907–"POSTFÖRSKOTT," which means COD, in imperf.

1907–"REMBOURSEMENT," in imperf.

1911–"Postförskott Rembousement" in perf and imperf.

1911-1920–As above, but with a number also printed on the stamp.

(REF#5560/73)

Labels and seals–letter seals

GERMANY 19??–Flying eagle and swastika

5 imperf LS4020

Vignette is of a flying eagle carrying or landing on a swastika. Each seal is a different color on silver–red, brown, orange, blue or green.

USA 1951–Christmas letter seals

16 rouletted LS4040 (photo)

Sheetlets of 24 stamps for use during the Christmas season included eight triangular labels–there were also four diamond shapes, eight triangular shapes, with one curved edge, and four other shaped labels. There are at least two different sheets, each multi-colored, one with each seal's border in green and the other with the border in flesh (salmon). The designs are the same in each sheet. The triangle designs are:

Vignette	Inscription
An eagle with outstretched wings holding holly branches.	NOEL
A flying airplane with cloud and star background.	HAPPY LANDING
A snow covered rural cottage.	None
A poinsettia.	None
A patriotic shield with 3 stars and 7 stripes.	GOD BLESS AMERICA
A silhouette of the Statue of Liberty in front of a circular area with 9 red stars.	HOLIDAY WISHES
A burning candle and pinecones.	None
Two bells and ribbons.	Holiday Greetings

Labels and seals–publicity-advertisements

These labels were issued to publicize a business or product. They typically do not include a date. Labels that advertise events are classified in the "publicity commemorative" grouping.

AUSTRALIA 1976–Benson & Hedges Air Race

1 perf LS5020

This item, produced in a sheetlet of four, commemorates the 1976 trans-Australian air race sponsored by Benson & Hedges. The design is of a biplane on a triangular background (REF#2300/35).

CANADA   **1979–Hinton Tourist Mail**
        20   **perf**   **LS5040**

Sheets of 20 different triangles were issued with green and red printing to commemorate and advertise an assortment of things. They are all inscribed with,"TOURIST MAIL SERVICE HINTON DERBY DAYS." Hinton, Alberta is a town of 5,000 people in the foothills of the Canadian Rockies, about 45 miles northeast of Jasper (REF#1005).

ETHIOPIA   **1979, 1982–Pro Foundation Economia**
        2   **imperf**   **LS5060**

The basic sheet has a reproduction of the three triangles Ethiopia issued in 1961 to commemorate the Emperor's 50th wedding anniversary and a $5 airmail issued in 1947 depicting the former capital. These reproductions are in the same colors and size as the original stamps, but are imperf. The sheet is printed in black with, "Pro Foundation Economia Ethiopia Price US $5 Debre Zeit, 1979." The second sheet is the first sheet overprinted in red with "Against the Hunger," "Minus 50%," and with "1982" and red bars on top of the "1979" date. These two souvenir sheets were not released by the government.

FRANCE   **1900–Panorama du Tour du Monde**
        1   **perf**   **LS5080**

In blue printing on white paper, the vignette is of an oriental building and inscribed, "PARIS 1900 PANORAMA DU TOUR DU MONDE."

        1930–Fondation Byrd
        1   **probably rouletted LS5100**

This multi-colored label depicts a portrait of Admiral Byrd with an airplane underneath. The inscription is "FRANCE AMERIQUE FONDATION BYRD" (REF#4116/144).

GERMANY   **?–Berlin - Eduard Dressler**
        1   **perf**   **LS5120 (photo)**

A yellow and blue item for "Eduard Dressler, Berlin S.W.," with a vignette of a square-shaped glue-pot.

        ?–?
        1   **imperf**   **LS5140**

On gold paper with a solid black background is an embossed inscription in gold "60JAHRE V7B. BARMEN" around the edge of a gold platter. Written across the gold platter in black script is "Capama." Also has "60" in each corner.

LS5120

LS5200

LS5220

LS5260

1924 to 1926–Stuttgart - JUGOSI
2   imperf   LS5160

On yellow paper with a solid black background is inscribed in yellow, "JUGOSI EDELM-ESSE STUTTGART" and a date in either 1924 or 1926.

1950–Oberammergau
1   rouletted   LS5180

This label is a gold foil triangular embossed with, "OBERAMMERGAU 1950." There is no printing on the label, just the embossing.

GREAT BRITAIN   Late 1940s–Land's End
1   perf   LS5200 (photo)

This label is printed primarily in orange and green. The border is depicted as heavy braided rope. The vignette is of a cottage with the sea in the background. The roof of the cottage is inscribed, "FIRST & LAST HOUSE IN ENGLAND." The caption "Land's End" also appears.

SALVADOR, EL   ?–Coffee promotion
1   perf   LS5220 (photo)

A green printed item with a vignette of a seated woman holding a cup of coffee with two coffee plants growing in the background. It is inscribed, "2 C REPUBLICA de el SALVADOR" and "USE SALVADOR COFFEE IT IS THE BEST GROWN" and "TOME CAFE DE EL SALVADOR ES EL MEJOR DEL MUNDO."

SOUTH AFRICA   ?–Oranges promotion
1   ?   LS5240

The inscription, "South African Oranges," is repeated three times in the border. The central vignette is of two oranges with green leaves and a mauve background. The label was overprinted in black with, "BUY THE EMPIRE'S FRUIT." (Was it issued without the overprint?)

1910–Capetown Historical Pageant
3   perf   LS5260 (photo)

These items replicate the central image from the Cape triangles, but have a simpler border style. The border inscription is, "HISTORICAL PAGENT OF SOUTH AFRICA CAPE-

TOWN OCT 1910." They were produced in red, blue or green. (Do other colors exist?) (REF# 8080/141).

SWITZERLAND(?)   ?–Europa Unity commemoratives
        3   perf   LS5280 (photo)

These labels come in either red, green, or blue on white paper. The image is of a raised hand carrying a flaming torch and is inscribed, "EUROPA UNITA FORTIS EST."

UNKNOWN   ?–Philips
        1   imperf   LS5300 (photo)

The vignette is of a black shape like a toilet-bowl plunger with "PHILUMA PHILIPS" in white lettering on a red background.

LS5280

LS5300

LS5320

LS5360

USA   ?–Allen Reproduction Co., Philadelphia
        1   imperf   LS5320 (photo)

With yellow lettering on black background this label has a letter "A" as large as the entire label. The rest of the inscription includes, "ALLEN REPRODUCTION COMPANY" and a Philadelphia, PA address and phone numbers.

?–DeBouzek Engraving Co., Salt Lake
        1   imperf   LS5340

This advertising label has a black background with turquoise lettering, "DE BOUZEK ENGRAVING COMPANY SALT LAKE," on five horizontal lines.

1909–WallaWalla, WA
        1   imperf   LS5360 (photo)

On a solid navy blue background is printed in white "What Walla Walla Wants is YOU."

1930s?–Mother's Day
        1   imperf   LS5380

The item has two-tone blue printing on white paper with the inscription, "Mothers Day–2nd Sunday in May–remember your mother with her favorite flowers–leave your order now."

1930s?–Esquire Magazine
1   imperf   LS5400

This item has red and white printing on black paper. Inscription is, "watch for our Christmas message in Esquire," plus a cartoon drawing of a man's face.

1947(?)–Boston Gift Show
1   imperf   LS5420

On a light blue background is dark blue and white printing in five horizontal lines, "SEE OUR EXHIBIT AT THE BOSTON GIFT SHOW SEPTEMBER 1-5 HOTEL STATLER."

1947–Salem Cherry Festival
1   rouletted   LS5440 (photo)

In red and green printing on white paper, these labels depict a cluster of cherries in front of a stylized building, (possibly the state capital of Oregon?) and inscribed, "JULY 17-18-19 1947 SALEM CHERRY FESTIVAL."

1956–Engineers Are People
1   perf   LS5460 (photo)

This advertising label was produced by the Helical Potentiometer Division of Beckman Instruments and sent in a Christmas package to its clients. This item is No. 1 of the set of five different items produced. The brown on yellow-brown vignette depicts a caveman making prehistoric cave drawings with the inscription, "ENGINEERS are PEOPLE." These were produced in sheets of 16 stamps (REF#7720/160).

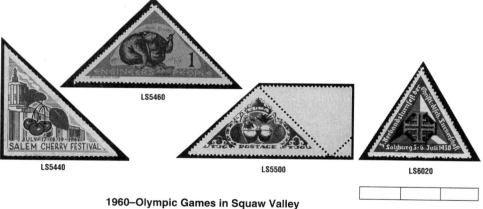

LS5460

LS5440   LS5500   LS6020

1960–Olympic Games in Squaw Valley
5   perf   LS5480

Two different triangular-shaped advertising labels were issued in connection with the Squaw Valley Winter Olympics. Each is inscribed with, "FOR TICKET INFORMATION WRITE OLYMPIC WINTER GAMES-SAN FRANCISCO." One vignette has an ice skater and skier depicted–colors red, blue, and white. These stamps come in two forms due to being produced in panes of labels–either a right-side imperf, or a left-side imperf. The other vignette is of the official emblem for these games in a white circle with pointed edging. This stamp comes in three forms–it has either two imperf edges, or a right-side imperf or left-side imperf (REF#1255/211).

1993–The Friends of Tuva
2   perf   LS5500 (photo)

These two labels were issued by the Friends of Tuva Society, for the country of Tana Tuva. The styling is similar to the old Tana Tuva stamps from the 1930s. One label is in red and the other in grey-green. The images are the same and are of a pair of hands playing two drums. They are denominated as "3 TUG."

Labels and seals–publicity-commemorative

These labels were issued to honor a particular event or happening. When issued after the event has happened, they are purely commemoratives. Typically they include a reference to a specific date or time period. When issued before and during an event, they were also for advertising purposes.

AUSTRIA   1930–Christian German Sports Association
1   perf   LS6020 (photo)

This label has a central vignette printed in red, black, gold and gray depicting a Jerusalem cross with the letters "C D T & O" attached to its arms. The border is gray with an inscription that translates to, "3rd Sports Festival of Christian German Sports Association" and "Salzburg 3-6 Juli 1930."

AUSTRIA/HUNGARY 1874–Arctic Expedition
3 or more   imperf   LS6040

In 1871, an Arctic expedition of Weyprecht and Payer conquered Mt. Isbjorn and in 1872, Mt. Tegethoff. These peaks are in Franz Josef Land, an Arctic archipelago of 187 islands, named for the Austrian emperor. In 1874, these two striking items were issued by Grillparzerverein to commemorate its accomplishments, with celebrations in Vienna and Budapest.

These items are embossed with wavy edges. The bottom border is inscribed, "26 SEPT–CAP WIEN–1874" on one, and "CAP BUDAPEST" on the other. The "Cap Wien" item is in yellow, red and navy. The "Cap Budapest" item is in purple and silver. There is also a "Cap Budapest" item in forest green on copper (or gold). And although I have no reference on it, I suspect there is also another "Cap Wien" item.

BELGIUM   1897–Brussels Exposition
1   perf   LS6060 (photo)

In black printing on white paper is the vignette of a seated, voluptuous woman, looking over a street scene of a block of buildings, autos, and pedestrians. The inscription is the name and address of a firm and "EXPOSITION 1897 BRUXELLES."

?–International Fair in Brussels
4   perf   LS6080 (photo)

Each label is in a different color–red, blue, purple, or dark green. The central vignettes are all the same–a large modern building with many, many pedestrians walking around in front of it. The borders are inscribed in four different languages, one per label, which says,

Country	Year	Item		Mint	Used	Cover
	No. in set	Separation	Item Number			
Description						

"INTERNATIONAL FAIR, BRUSSELS in APRIL 1st till 3rd WEDNESDAY GREAT WORLD-WIDE MARKET."

CANADA   **1920–Fairs in B.C.**

            1   rouletted   **LS6100 (photo)**

    This label publicizes three different fairs held in British Columbia in 1920. The center is a red triangle inscribed with a white, "1920 FAIRS." Each border has the name of a city and the dates of the fair in that city. The cities are Vancouver, Victoria and New Westminster. The fairs covered the period from Sept. 11 to Oct. 2.

LS6100

LS6140

LS6120

LS6200

            1967–Confederation Centennial

            1   rouletted   **LS6120 (photo)**

    The image is of an outline map of Canada in blue printing with a red and white flag of Canada in the center. In the two bottom corners are the portraits of MacDonald, the prime minister in 1867, and Pearson, the prime minister in 1967. It is inscribed, "LE CENTENAIRE DA LA CONFEDERATION."

FINLAND   **1951–Wakefield Air Cup**

            1   perf   **LS6140 (photo)**

    This label, with brown printing on white paper, depicts a model airplane and a trophy. It is inscribed, "1951 WAKEFIELD SUOMI FINLAND."

GERMANY   **1901–Potsdam**

            1   imperf   **LS6160**

    In blue printing on white paper is a Germanic crest in white, with white lettering of, "PROVINZIAL OBST AUSSTELLUNG–POTSDAM–28.SEPT–2.OKTB,1901."

            1905–Kornerbund

            1   imperf   **LS6180**

    In red printing on white paper are crossed swords and some fancy initials in white, with white lettering "5.2.1905 Kornerbund."

Country	Year	Item		Mint	Used	Cover
	No. in set	Separation	Item Number			
Description						

1911–Cologne
1   perf   LS6200 (photo)

This is a larger item with red and dark green printing on a white background inscribed, "VERBANDSTAG IN COLN A/RH 5-7 AUGUST 1911" and the initials "VDH" in a circular wreath. Also has the symbol for physicians.

1912–Esperanto Congress
1   imperf   LS6220

In green printing on white paper is the Esperanto star and two heraldic shields. Border inscription in white is, "VII GERMANA ESPERANTA KONGRESO– DANZIG 27.7-1.8.1912 ZOPPOT."

1925–Krefeld
2   imperf   LS6240 (photo)

On either red or orange paper with a solid black background is an embossed inscription in either red or orange, "VOM 3-10 MAI 1925 KREFELDER VERKEHRS: UND HEIMAT-WOCHE." This translates to "Krefeld (a city in Germany) Traffic and Home Week May 3-10, 1925."

LS6240

LS6280

LS6300

LS6320

1956–Frankfurter Bookfair
1   imperf   LS6260

This item has a black and white logo that looks like two open books on an orange background. It has "FRANKFURTER BUCHMESSE 1956 19-24 SEPT" in black lettering.

1962–Markkleeberg
2   imperf   LS6280 (photo)

The multi-colored central vignette is of a ship's mast with banners and flags flying from it. The border in light or medium blue is inscribed in dark blue, "10.LANDWIRTSCHAFTS AUSSTELLUNG DDR MARKKLEEBERG JUNI-JULI 1962." This translates to, "10th Agricultural Exhibition Markkleeberg, East Germany, June-July 1962."

1959–Dirigible flight Leipzig Dresden KMS
1   imperf   LS6300 (photo)

This label was used for a dirigible flight from Karl-Marx-Stadt to Leipzig to Dresden and back to Karl-Marx-Stadt from April 4-12, 1959. The vignette is of a dirigible in red on a blue

Country	Year	Item		Mint	Used	Cover
	No. in set	Separation	Item Number			
Description						

background with the border inscribed   in red, "Karl-Marx-Stadt–Leipzig–Dresden–Karl-Marx-Stadt Baumgarten–Gedenkflug zur 2. Sachsenschau." It is printed on white paper.

HOLLAND   1937–Wereld (Scouting) Jamboree
          1   imperf   LS6320 (photo)

A triangular label issued for the 1935 World Scouting Jamboree in Holland. Design has Scouting symbol at apex of triangle with inscription, "NEDERLANDSCHE POSTZEGEL-CENTRALE STAND 14 WERELDJAMBOREE 1937 HOLLAND" (REF#1430/30).

HUNGARY   1921–Beekeeping
          3   imperf   LS6340 (photo)

These labels were printed in red or purple or blue on white paper. The image is of a bee with the border inscription, "DUNANTULI MEHESZETI KIALLITAS GYOR, 1921 AUGUSZ-TUS 14-15 (VAROSI KERESK. ISKOLA)."

          1925–Jokai Centennariuma
          3   perf   LS6360 (photo)

In grape, green, and carmine, one color per label is the vignette of a seated man in long robes, coat and helmet with a stringed musical instrument. It is inscribed, "1825-1925 JOKAI CENTENNARIUMA PETOFI TARSASAG."

          1926–MOHACS 400 years
          9   perf   LS6380 (photo)

This 400-year commemorative issue depicts a tall stone memorial tower with two bands of people carrying flags on each side of the tower. The border is inscribed, "NEMZETI-NAGYLÉTÜNK NAGY TEMETÖJE: 1526 MOHÁCS 1926." There are two basic color styles–one has red borders and one has blue borders. The border lettering and paper color are white. The vignette is in the following colors: for the blue borders, dark blue, orange, brown, red, black, green, and purple; for the red borders, green, blue. (I have seen nine of these items, but suspect there were at least 14 different items. Do you have others?)

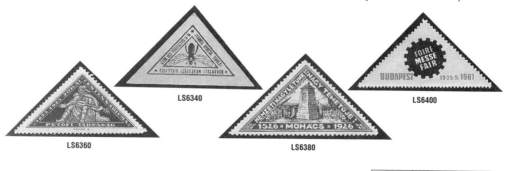

LS6360   LS6340   LS6380   LS6400

          1961–Budapest fair
          1   perf   LS6400 (photo)

This yellow label has a black gear design inscribed, "FOIRE MESSE FAIR." The background is inscribed, "BUDAPEST 19-29.5. 1961."

1968–UTASELLATO
1   perf   LS6420 (photo)

On a pale blue background is a large white number "20" over two golden branches with a gold inscription, "UTASELLATO 1948 1968."

LS6500   LS6420   LS6520   LS6540

INDIA   1964–Eucharistic Congress
1   imperf   LS6440

This imperf item depicts an Air India jet in front of some (unrecognized) symbol. The border inscription is, "INTERNATIONAL EUCHARISTIC CONGRESS 1964 AIR INDIA." (Can anyone supply me with the colors used?)

ITALY   1960–Olympic Games in Rome
7   imperf   LS6460

These labels were printed in sheets of six–three tete-beche pairs–all with the same design. The vignette has a glider at the apex, the Olympic rings in the middle and a landscape at the bottom. The border text is "POSTSEGELFLUG ELCHINGEN-HAHNENWEIDE ZUM OLYMPIA-JAHR 1960." The sheets come in seven different colors: black, red, blue, green, purple, orange, and gray (REF#1255/224).

JAPAN   1964–Olympic Games in Tokyo
1   perf   LS6480

This label has Greek text around the border that translates to, "The Hero's sacrifice is accepted by society as a gift." The vignette has a large central red circle inscribed "TOKYO 1964" over the Olympic rings printed in five colors. The rest of the stamp is an olive-gold color. It was issued as a souvenir sheet of 12 stamps, with the stamps making two hexagons, joined at the center (REF#1255/280).

SWEDEN   1958–World Football Championship
4   perf   LS6500 (photo)

This pink and brick red label has four different football-player vignettes, each with the green Esperanto star. The inscription in Esperanto is "8-29 junio 1958 MONDA CAMPIONECO SVEDUJO." They were printed as mini-sheets of the four different labels.

UKRAINE   1907-1909–labels issued while occupied
5   imperf   LS6520 (photo)

In 1907, during the Austrian occupation, a commemorative set of four triangulars was issued to celebrate the League of the Christian Germans in the area around Lvov. These depict a man with a pouch of seed he's sowing by throwing out handfuls while walking through a field. The four denominations and colors are 2h with black, red and gold; 10h in red; 20h in cepia; and 50h in yellow.

In 1909, while still under Austrian occupation, a 5h item, printed in black, red and golden, was issued for the same purpose in the Chernivici area. The vignette is of three young faces looking at a sunrise (REF#3350; #8320/Nov. 92).

UNKNOWN 1942–"Sandoz"

2 perf and imperf LS6540 (photo)

This label commemorates a 25-year period of providing medicine. The vignette is of a "superman" emblem in the center and two stalks of some kind of plant in a pale green and yellow design. The border has blue printing inscribed, "QUINQUE ET VIGINTI ANNI MEDICAMENTORUM "SANDOZ" MCMXVII-MCMXLII." (Was this created for the large Sandoz pharmaceutical firm?)

1972–?

1 imperf LS6560

On top of a background of a green, gray and red outline of a country(?) is inscribed, "PUEBLA CIUDAD FERIA 21 de Abril al 15 de Mayo 72" in black lettering.

USA 1950–World Ski Championship

1 imperf LS6580 (photo)

In red and blue printing on white paper is the vignette of a skier. Inscription includes, "FEBRUARY 13-19, 1950 ASPEN COLO. WORLD SKI CHAMPIONSHIP."

LS6580

LS6600

LS7020

LS7040

1971–Peshtigo Fire

1 roulette LS6600 (photo)

This gray, red, yellow and black printing of a stylized forest fire on white paper commemorates the 100th anniversary of a deadly forest fire. Its border reads, "1871 OCTOBER 8 1971 PESHTIGO, WISCONSIN AMERICA'S MOST DISASTROUS FOREST FIRE."

Labels and seals–publicity-propaganda

CROATIA 1953–"Free Croatia"

48 perf and imperf LS7020 (photo)

Country	Year	Item		Mint	Used	Cover
	No. in set	Separation	Item Number			
Description						

In the early 1950s, several sets of stamps were issued to support a "Free Croatia" movement. They were apparently produced by a "government in exile." However, their character raises questions about the "officialness" of the items–half of them do not even signify a (supposed) currency. They could easily be classified as a "bogus" item.

Their bottom border is inscribed with, "N.D. HRVATSKA," and the denomination–just like the postage stamps of Croatia. However, there were no triangular postage stamps issued by Croatia, so any triangulars with the "N.D. HRVATSKA" inscription are these Cinderella items. (Reference #8380 has a very informative two-page article specifically on the Croatia Exile issues.)

The four sets are as follows:

Subject	Number in set	Denominations
Flowers	6	5, 10, 20, 30, 40, 50
Flowers	6	5kn, 10kn, 20kn, 30kn, 40kn, 50kn
Birds	6	10, 20, 30, 40, 50, 60
Birds	6	35kn, 40kn, 45kn, 50kn, 60kn, 80kn

There are six different vignettes for the flowers, and six for the birds. The background colors vary between the two flower sets; likewise for the bird sets. Each set comes in both perf and imperf forms (REF#7420-1961/29;-1974/59; #7930/79; #8380/18).

GERMANY ?–Liberal Party seal
1 perf LS7040 (photo)

Printed in orange and black on white paper is a vignette of a large old oak tree with two shields at its base. One shield has a heraldic lion on it. The other has the text in German that translates to,"Justice is the foundation for the State. That is why we need proportional representation." There is also a bottom inscription,"Liberale 2pf Arbeitsge meinschaft," which refers to the Liberal (Party) Working Group.

GREAT BRITAIN Early 1970s–KERNOW issues
2 perf LS7060 (photo)

These were issued by a political movement for a "Free Cornwall," the most southern county of England. The vignette is of a plant growth, printed in black and ochre, with thorns reaching into each corner of the isosceles triangle. On the gray background is inscribed in black "KERNOW." It also comes with an overprint, "POSTYYS YN," and the inscription, "Posted in Cornwall," under the design.

LS7060   LS7080   LS7100   LS7120

IRELAND 1956–"One Flag-One Country" set
7 imperf LS7080 (photo)

These labels were issued to promote a united Ireland, one free from British "rule" in Northern Ireland. Possibly they were also for fund-raising.

There were four stamps in the initial issue, with each stamp having a separate design. They all have a green bottom border with a white inscription, "FREE IRELAND." The two borders around the apex are inscribed in green, "ONE FLAG ONE COUNTRY." They come in denominations of 1, 2, 3, and 4. There are four different vignettes, with each stamp using the colors red, green and orange.

The second issue is of three items–the denomination 3 was not printed. The inscriptions and vignettes are the same as the initial series; however, the colors are different–no orange was used, and the border areas are printed in red rather than green (REF#7420-1961/129).

NORWAY   1910–anti-alcohol
                1   perf   LS7100 (photo)

In ultramarine blue printing on white paper is a portrait of Asbjorn Kloster with the inscription, "BORT MED RUSDRIKKENE," (Away with intoxicating drinks) (REF#8320/Sep. 88).

RMS   1950s–Republic Maluku Selatan
                26   perf   LS7120 (photo)

In 1950, two South Moluccas islands rebelled against the Indonesian government in an attempt to gain independence. Numerous issues were made to (ostensibly) raise funds for the movement. They were labeled with, "REPUBLIK MALUKU SELATAN." The movement died along with its instigator in 1955.

There were three triangular sets as follows:

Year	Subject	Number in set	Denominations
1952	Butterflies	6	2K, 3K, 5K, 7-1/2, 10K, 12-1/2K, all with "POS POSTAGE"
1953	Fish	16	1K, 2K, 2-1/2K, 3K, 4K, 5K, 7-1/2, 10K, 12-1/2K, 15K, 17- 1/2K, 20K, 22-1/2K, 25K, 30K, 35K, all with wording "POS POSTAGE"
1954	Butterflies	4	5K, 7-1/2K, 10K, 12-1/2K, all with wording "POS UDARA"

(REF#7420-Jan. 62/11; #7630/13; #7930/79)

UKRAINE   1929-1931–labels issued while occupied
                2   imperf   LS7140

During the Russian occupation in 1929 and 1931, two propaganda labels were issued to promote camaraderie for the new members joining the Pioneer's organization in the Ukraine. One label, printed in red, blue, black and cream depicts a boy in short-sleeved shirt and shorts carrying a flag. The other, printed in red and black, has a similar vignette (REF#3350).

Labels and seals–world wars-Delandre

FRANCE   1914–Delandre seals
                5   rouletted   LS8020 (photo)

During World War I, a man named Delandre produced a considerable number of "charity" seals. Some were legitimate, but it appears many were not–they were a money-making scheme for himself. Regardless, he produced some very interesting philatelic items.

The designs, shapes and sizes were whatever different artists created. However, there is a consistent design "feel" in the type of graphics and colors used. The items were arranged on sheets, with an image being on the sheet only once. Odd-sized blank spaces occurred between the items since the seals were not of a standard size. Then somehow the sheets were (usually) rouletted.

Schmidt Catalog Number	Inscription
26	"?RESSE 26 d' Inf" in circle at apex of stamp. Vignette is a sculpture of a marching soldier with a bayoneted rifle slung over his shoulder.
77	"77 Régiment d' Infanterie," with the vignette primarily the Egyptian Sphinx.
1240	Apex contains "20," bottom panel has "1914" and "1916" at each end with "PYRAMIDES 1798 IENA 1806 FRIEDLAND1807 ALBUFERA 1811" with a vignette of multiple horses' heads.
1364.1 and 1364.2	The number "4" is in the apex. Vignette is of the Egyptian Sphinx and a pyramid with a piece of field artillery in each of the lower corners.

(REF#4800)

LS8020   LS8020

Labels and seals–world wars-other military

HOLLAND/G.B. 1943–Dutch Field Post Letter Seal
4 perf and imperf LS9020

The Royal Netherlands Brigade in England in June of 1943 issued 280,000 letter seals depicting Minerva in blue on a vermilion background with white inscriptions. This image is the same as used on the 1936 Netherlands six cent postal issue. The inscription is in English, "DUTCH FIELD POST LETTER SEAL," or in Dutch, "NEDERLANDSCHE VELDPOST SLUIT ZEGEL," with the two languages alternating on a sheet of 28 stamps. They were made in both perf and imperf forms (REF#466).

USA 1917–Patriotic seal
1 imperf LS9040

This Delandre-style item has a multi-colored vignette of three figures: a standing woman holding the American flag in one hand and a wreath in the other; a kneeling soldier with a bayoneted rifle; and a kneeling farm worker with a scythe and sheaf of grain. The border is inscribed, "SERVICE TOGETHER."

Labels and seals–world wars-patriotic

USA 1940–patriotic label
1 rouletted LS10020 (photo)

This pre-World War II label has a blue center with "1940" in white, and a red border inscribed in white, "BANISH POVERTY RESTORE LIBERTY PRODUCTION FOR USE." It also has in tiny black printing, "Copyright 1936 by Mima & Lampell PO Box 394 Billings Montana."

LS10020   LS10060   LS10120

LS10100

194?–Mrs. Churchill's Fund
1   imperf   LS10040

This embossed silver foil label depicts the portrait of a bulldog in blue on a field of red and blue stripes as though the portrait was over the center of the Union Jack, the flag of Great Britain. It has a red inscription, "MRS CHURCHILL'S FUND."

1942–victory labels
5   imperf   LS10060

These labels were issued to urge Americans to buy War Bonds. All five items have the same design–a large blue V surrounding a waving American flag in red, white, and blue. The five items each have a different inscription printed on three horizontal lines in blue as follows:

- "KEEP 'EM FLYING BUY U.S. BONDS"
- "YOU CAN HELP BUY U.S. BONDS"
- "BUY A SHARE OF FREEDOM"
- "KEEP 'EM ROLLING BUY U.S. BONDS"
- "REMEMBER PEARL HARBOR"

(REF#7900/Feb. 42)

1942–victory labels
1   imperf   LS10080

This label was issued to urge Americans in the War Effort. Printed in red and blue, this item is a single large "V" with the inscription covering the entire label, "The One Test for Every Decision WILL IT HELP TO WIN THE WAR" (REF#7900/Dec. 42).

194?–victory labels
2   imperf and roulettedLS10100 (photo)

A large red, white, and blue "V" encloses the word "victory" repeated 3 times and .".-" with two stars in the center (.".-" is Morse code for the letter "V"). One item is imperf and the other is rouletted.

194?–victory labels - NY Savings Banks
2   imperf   LS10120 (photo)

Country	Year	Item		Mint	Used	Cover
	No. in set	Separation	Item Number			
Description						

These two items are inscribed with, "Save for victory" with large "V" and a circular seal that says, "THE SAVINGS BANKS OF NEW YORK STATE." One is printed in red and one in blue.

Labels and seals–world wars-Swiss Army

There were more than 2,300 different items issued by individual units of the Swiss Army to raise charitable funds, including aid to soldiers' families. Some were issued for World War I, but most were during World War II. The stamps were not used to pay for postage, since a soldier's mail was sent as free mail. However, the stamps were made to be easily recognizable, so the postal workers could give the mail a higher priority service. Since they did not need canceling, the mail could be processed faster once it was recognized as being from a military unit.

The stamp's designs are varied, but they typically used bold graphic styles. Although they were typically perforated, most also exist in imperf form. In a few cases, the imperfs were more plentiful.

SWITZERLAND	1914-1945–Swiss Army Stamps		
	52	perf and imperf	LS11020 (photo)

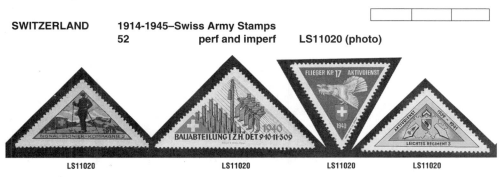

LS11020   LS11020   LS11020   LS11020

The table below includes the stamp's inscription to aid in identification of the item.

Group	Sulser No.	Inscription
1914/18 3.Division	135	3.DIVISION. GEB.-BRIGADE 9
	136	STAB GEBIRGS-J.-BRIGADE 9
	137	STAB GEBIRGS-J.-BATAILLON 35
	138	GEBIRGS-J.-REGIMENT 17
	139	GEBIRGS-J.-BATAILLON 89
	140	GEBIRGS-JNFANTERIE-KP.II/35
	141	GEBIRGS-MITRAILLEUR-KP.I/1
	142	GEBIRGS-MITRAILLEUR-KP.II/18
	143	SIGNAL-PIONIER-KOMPANIE 2
	144	FELDPOST DER 3.DIVISION
1939/45 Boulangers	16	BÄCKER KP.13
Feldpost	7	P.Camp.Br.Mont.10 Service Actif 1939-40
Aviation	81	FLIEGER KP.17 AKTIVDIENST 1939-blue, pink, red
	82	FLIEGER KP.17 AKTIVDIENST 1939-black 1940 overprint
	83	FLIEGER KP.17 AKTIVDIENST 1940-green, pink, red
	84	FLIEGER KP.17 AKTIVDIENST 1940-black 1945 overprint
Guetteurs	34	FL.BEOB.GR.12

Group	Sulser No.	Inscription
Troupes frontieres	107	GRENZ-FÜS.KP.I/243 GRENZBESETZUNG 1939 FÜR UNSERE SOLDATEN
	108	(information missing)
	109	(information missing)
	164	GZ.FÜS.KP.III/269 AKTIVDIENST 1940 +WIR WACHEN+ - red, blue, black
	165	GZ.FÜS.KP.III/269 AKTIVDIENST 1940 +WIR WACHEN+ - overprint "Grenzdienst 1941"
	172	GZ.FÜS.KP.II/285 AKTIVDIENST 1940
Service construction	5	BAUABTEILUNG I Z.H.DET.9-10-11-309-
	6	BAUABTEILUNG I Z.H.DET.9-10-11-309-overprint 1941
	7	BAUABTEILUNG I Z.H.DET.9-10-11-309-overprint 1942-1943
Infanterie	427	FÜS.BAT. 97
	437	AKTIVDIENST 1940 FÜS.BAT. 104 NIT LUGG LAN-gray, red, blue, brown, black
	438	AKTIVDIENST 1940 FÜS.BAT.104 NIT LUGG LAN- overprint 1943
	439	AKTIVDIENST 1940 FÜS.BAT. 104 NIT LUGG LAN- gray violet, red, blue, brown, black
	440	AKTIVDIENST 1940 FÜS.BAT. 104 NIT LUGG LAN-green, red, blue, brown, black
	441	AKTIVDIENST 1940 FÜS.BAT. 104 NIT LUGG LAN-yellow, red, blue, brown, black
	445	Füs.Bat. 104 Stabs-Kp. - white paper
	446	Füs.Bat. 104 Stabs-Kp. - yellow paper
	47	Füs.Bat. 105(5.Division)
Troupes legeres	8	LEICHTE BRIGADE 3 - yellow, black
	9	LEICHTE BRIGADE 3 - gold, black
	10	AKTIVDIENST 1939-1941 LEICHTES REGIMENT 3
	11	AKTIVDIENST 1939-1941 LEICHTES REGIMENT 3 - overprint 1944
	12	Stab L.Rgt. 3
Troupes motorisees	7	MOBILISATION 1939 MOTFZ.-REP.ABT.3-red, blue, dark violet
	8	MOBILISATION 1939 MOTFZ.-REP.ABT.3-red, black
	11	1939/40MOT.MITR.KP.4-red, black, grey, yellow
	12	1939/40MOT.MITR.KP.4-red, black, bluegreen, yellow
Pontonniers	7	PONT.LASTW.KOL.2 AKTIVDIENST 1940
	8	PONTONIER KOMP.III/2
Cyclistes	1	MOB 39-40 BAT.CYC.1 - blue, black, red, green
	2	MOB 39-40 BAT.CYC.1 - grey, black, red, green
	44	AKTIVDIENST RDF.KP.34 1939
Sappeurs	51	SAP.BAT.23 1939
Troupes territoriales	246	Ter.Füs.Kp.II/154 - brownish carmine, gray, black
	247	TER.FÜS.KP.II/154 - red, gray, black

(REF#5465; #7120/29; #7180/45)

Locals–modern

Locals are stamps issued for use within a small area–a city, town, or over a limited route. They usually were established to fill a void left by the governmental services in the

Country	Year	Item		Mint	Used	Cover
	No. in set	Separation	Item Number			
Description						

surrounding areas. These stamps were issued by a private person, a firm and by municipalities to use in the pre-payment of the fee for transporting mail in areas not covered by any governmental service.

Local post stamps were affixed to a letter, along with the proper postage for the country whose mail service would be used for the rest of the delivery. The local post usually took the mail from some unserviced remote location and delivered it to a governmental post office for inclusion in the traditional mail service. Some local post operations picked up mail from the governmental post office and provided a local delivery service, which was paid for by the use of the stamp upon delivery–a COD-type of operation.

Most governments run their country's postal operations and usually do not permit private competition. Where permitted, local post services often had requirements for their stamps to be distinct from the postage stamps for the country they are within.

In recent decades, there has been a type of "local post" label arise, which is not related to the provision of a mail service. These are labels issued by individuals for "make-believe" delivery services–they are "vanity labels." They are used on mail and have many of the characteristics of artistamps. However, unlike true artistamps, which have never gone through a postal delivery, these modern locals are intended to be used on mail to friends, acquaintances and others interested in locals. The items below are associated with some form of postal service or include an inscription alluding to a local post.

BAHAMAS **1971–Grand Bahamas Island Local Post**
1 imperf L1020

In 1971, this Bahamas-based service issued an item in black printing on green paper inscribed, "LOCAL POST GBI AAF-IRC-" on the border and "APRIL 2, 1959 PROJECT MERCURY ASTRONAUTS SELECTED" as the design; 500 were issued (REF#1292).

1982–Chub Cay Carrier Service
2 imperf L1040

In 1982, this service issued stamps for its mail handling services on Chub Cay, which does not have a post office. The three-square-mile island with about 56 permanent inhabitants is a long and narrow piece of land. The "carrier" for this service was the local taxi driver. The triangular stamp is for local delivery. It is a 50-cent denomination in blue and green inscribed, "CHUB CAY CARRIER SERVICE–LOCAL DELIVERY," with the design being a map of the island. Two non-triangular stamps are used for domestic and international delivery. There is also a souvenir sheet which contains all three stamps (REF#8860; #8440vol. 11-3/18-19).

GREAT BRITAIN **1954–Herm Island**
12 perf L1060 (photo)

One of the British Channel islands famous for its local post stamps, Herm issued a set of 12 triangulars in 1954. These depict Herm's flora and fauna in bright colors. They are inscribed simply, "HERM ISLAND." There are 12 different designs, each with its own denomination. The stamps are perforated. There are proofs in imperforate form. (REF#161; #8200/102).

1955–Herm Island bisect
1 perf L1080

Country	Year	Item		Mint	Used	Cover
	No. in set	Separation	Item Number			
Description						

For four days in August of 1955, the eight doubles triangular was bisected and used for the four doubles rate on postcards. About 5,000 were used (REF#8200/102).

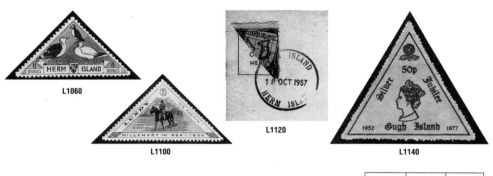

L1060

L1120

L1100

L1140

1955 and 1961–Lundy
19   perf stamps and
**   imperf mini-sheet   L1100 (photo)**

Since 1929, the little island of Lundy, off the coast of Britain, has issued local post stamps for its delivery service to the mainland.

In 1955, it issued two sets of triangulars–one set is six different designs of birds in denominations of 1/2, 1, 2, 4, 6, and 9. They are inscribed, "LUNDY MILLENARY 954 1954 AIR MAIL"; the other set is of horses, comes in the same denominations and the same inscription without "airmail."

In 1961, the horse designs were reprinted in different colors than the 1955 set, the inscriptions are all in black, and they were overprinted with "Europa 1961." (Note: although these stamps are perforated, there were proofs made in imperf form.) Also in 1961, a miniature sheet of the Europa stamps was produced, but here the items are printed in different colors than the 1961 individual stamps, the inscriptions are not in black, and the sheet is imperforate (REF#4151/33; #8920/66[general background on Lundy]).

1957–Herm Island bisects
2   perf   L1120 (photo)

Near the end of the summer of 1957, for a one-month period, the 1-penny Herm stamp, depicting the island on a nautical map, was cut to form a diagonal bisect. This was used on postcards and until a new supply of the 1/2-penny stamps arrived from the printers.

1977–Gugh Island
6   perf and imperf   L1140 (photo)

Gugh Island issued a perf and an imperf set each of three items–a stamp in gold, a stamp in silver and a souvenir sheet in both gold and silver celebrating Queen Elizabeth's Silver Jubilee. They are inscribed, "Silver Jubilee Gugh Island," have a portrait of the Queen, and a 50p denomination.

QUAITI STATE IN HADHRAMAUT–1968
44   perf   L1160 (photo)

This sultanate in eastern Aden, one of a group of 13 Arabian "places" which the FIP found in late 1967, was heavily involved in issuing non-postally valid items. They were placed on the list of items and "countries" banned from FIP exhibitions. See the section on Black Blots in Chapter 5. For this reason, they are listed here as Cinderella items.

These items all are inscribed with "QUAITI STATE IN HADHRAMAUT."

Year	Subject	Number of items
1968	Animals	14
1968	Seven Wonders of the World	14
1968	Mexico City Olympics	8
1968	Antique planes and modern rockets	8

L1160

L1180

L1220

USA   **1953–Shrub Oak, New York**
           1   roulette   L1180 (photo)

Herman Herst Jr. created this first modern triangular U.S. local to get acceptance from the U.S. Postal Service of a stamp that would not be confused with the normal U.S. postage. The U.S. Code permits local post operation for areas not served by the Postal Service. It also requires appropriate U.S. postage be used. With rectangular-shaped locals, the Postal Service was concerned it might not be able to quickly tell when the appropriate U.S. stamps were being used. Thus, Herman created a triangular-shaped stamp.

The central design is of three oak trees, printed in green on white paper. The border inscription in red is "SHRUB OAK (N.Y.) LOCAL POST TWO CENTS." The initial issue on May 1, 1953, was a printing of 96,000 stamps (REF#7480/11; #7780-1961/73; #8260).

1953-1961–Brook Hill Local Service, Wisconsin
           5   imperf   L1200 (photo)

During a 14-year period of operation, this service issued five different triangular items.

1) The June 1953 issue is red and black printing on buff paper inscribed in the center , "TO SPEED MAIL FROM GENESEE DEPOT WISCONSIN AFTER P.O. IS CLOSED A BROOKHILL LOCAL SERVICE," and a border inscription, "POSTED AT WALES, WIS. –POSTED AT WAUKESHA, WIS. –POSTED AT OCONOMOWOC"; 2,000 were issued.
2) The 1954 issue was of the same color, design and inscription as above, but in a slightly smaller size; 6,000 were issued.
3) In 1956, the prior design, inscriptions and printing colors were used on green paper with a big bold red "10" overprint. Again, 6,000 were issued.
4) In 1958, the same item as #3 was issued on orange (goldenrod) paper, again in an issue of 6,000.
5) In 1961, a whole new design was used. This shows a map of the four cities mentioned on the earlier stamps printed in black and red on yellow ungummed paper. The cities are still inscribed on the border, but without "POSTED AT." This was also overprinted with a big red "10" and had an issuance of 6,000. Note that this is the only one of the issues that was not done on gummed paper stock.

(REF#7780-1961/23,109; #1292)

1954–Centerport Local Service, New York
           2   imperf   L1220 (photo)

In 1954, this Centerport, N.Y. service issued a rectangular stamp with roulette separations. The design was completely a triangular design and a very significant one. The USPS had ruled a previous local post stamp to be in violation of the postal regulations since it contained the word "POST" and could be confused with a regular postage stamp. The Post Office Department ruled a triangular image was sufficiently unlike regular U.S. stamps and could be used. Mr. Schmitt, operator of the local service, used the rouletting for easy separation and used the triangular design to meet postal regulations.

The design was printed in blue on white paper and depicts an outline map of Long Island on top of an old ship anchor and rope. It has a border inscription, "CENTERPORT L.I., New York LOCAL SERVICE." Some 5,000 were issued.

A second triangular issue was produced, but never officially put into service. It is printed in red and blue and depicts the same map and anchor image with the word "CENTERPORT" at the top of the design. Its border inscription is simply, "LOCAL SERVICE"; 10,000 were made.

The service had a life of about two years and was closed due to pressure from local postal authorities. At that time, the residents of Centerport had no delivery service and had to pick up their mail from the post office (REF#7780-1961/151; #1292).

L1200	L1200	L1240

1956-1961–Sandia Crest, New Mexico
1   perf   L1240 (photo)

Sandia Crest is a mountain top in New Mexico more than 10,600 feet high. A local post service was established to serve the customers of a curio shop at the mountain's peak. The design depicts the crest with a cloud above it and the text ,"ELEVATION 10,678 FEET," printed in yellow on white gummed paper. The border, printed in black, has the inscription, "SANDIA CREST NEW MEXICO LOCAL DELIVERY," with a 2-cent denomination in the two lower corners. These were printed in sheetlets of four stamps, with a total issue of 10,000 (REF#7780April 62/29).

1962-1973–Fort Findlay Local Post, Findlay, Ohio
5   roulette   L1260 (photo)

From 1962-1973, this local service in Findlay, Ohio, had five triangular issues.

1) The first 1962 issue depicted an old-time wooden log fort with a 10-cent denomination and inscribed in the border inscription, "FORT FINDLAY LOCAL POST FINDLAY OHIO," in brown and green; 2,476 were issued in sheets of 16–four blocks of four stamps.
2) Later in 1962, the same stamp was issued with a green wreath and red 5-cent overprint; 2,064 were issued.
3) In 1969, the design became an outline map of the USA with the same inscription, but not in the border. This was a 10-cent denomination in blue and red, and about 1,200 were issued.
4) In 1973, a commemorative for 150 years of U.S. Postal Service in Findlay was issued in red and blue with a 10-cent denomination; 1,600 were issued.
5) In 1974, the item in 3) was overprinted in blue with "FLAG CITY 1974." About 400 were issued. (REF#1292; #7780Jan64/15)

1964–Mountainville Local Pony Post, Utah
1   imperf   L1280

Country	Year	Item			Mint	Used	Cover
	No. in set	Separation	Item Number				
Description							

This short-lived local post operated for only two days during the UTAPEX 1964 show. The Philatelic Society of Utah issued 1,000 of these brown on yellow paper with the inscription, "MOUNTAINVILLE TO MOUNT PLEASANT LOCAL PONY POST," in a 35-cent denomination. The "pony" in the inscription refers to the use of horseback to carry the mail between the two points. The design is of a natural arch rock formation (Utah's Arch Rock) and a small horse and rider (REF#1292; #7240/776).

1966–Satellite Beach Local Post, Florida
3   imperf   L1290

These locals were printed on three different paper colors–red, green and blue. They have a 10-cent denomination with a design about the Test Ban Treaty (REF#3480).

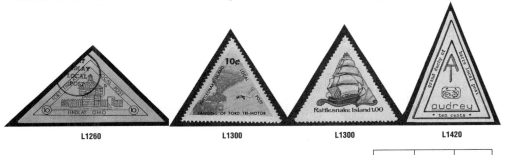

L1260   L1300   L1300   L1420

1967-1989(?)–Rattlesnake Island, Ohio
134   perf and imperf   L1300 (photo)

Ten miles north of Port Clinton, Ohio, in Lake Erie is Rattlesnake Island. This is a small island, only 85 acres, but it is big in its contribution to local post philatelics. In 1966, the U.S. Postal Service did not provide a pickup or delivery to the Island, so a local service was started. The Post Office Department then ruled that Rattlesnake Island's use of rectangular stamps was likely to be confused with the required U.S. postage, even though the locals were not placed on the upper right corner per Post Office requirements. This led the service's operators to design a triangular issue. The U.S. had never used that shape and it was clearly distinctive and would not be confused with normal postage.

The use of the triangular shape continued from then until the end of the service. In each year three different vignettes were issued and these were produced in both perf and imperf forms.

Also of note is a souvenir sheet issued by Uganda in 1994. This sheet depicts the Ford Tri-motor airplane used by Island Airways, the carrier for the Rattlesnake Island locals, and two of the early local post stamps. See the entry in the Postage Stamps Listings in the Stamps-on-Stamps section.

Year	Subject
67	Map, plane, scene (10,000 issued)
68	Gulls, pheasant, aoudads (20,000 issued)
69	Sailing race, lake schooner, island sunset (20,000 issued)
70	Flowers
71	Island views
72	Sports–fishing, tennis, sightseeing, and two of a monument (eight stamps issued)
73	Fish
74	Blue jay, bluebird, woodpecker

Year	Subject
75	Butterflies
76	Flags
77	Birds–goldfinch, indigo bunting, cardinal
78	Battleships
79	Animals–squirrel, raccoon, badger
80	Insects
81	Eire Indian culture
82	Ducks
83	Marina, lighthouse, recreation center
84	Wildflowers–trout lily, white trillium, wild aster
85	Wildlife–fox squirrel, white-tailed deer, wild turkey
86	Canada goose, herring gull, heron
86	$2 triplane 20th anniversary–a fourth stamp in this year
87	Shipping–the "Niagara," ore carrier, pleasure craft ($1, $1.5, $2 denomination)
88	Lighthouses
89	Owls

(REF#8260; #7390/402)

1969–Texas Letter Express
2   **imperf**   **L1320**

One item is a green U.N. Seal on white paper in a 10-cent denomination, with 250 is-sued. The other item is a 5-cent denomination for postcard use of a red Dove and Letter on white paper with 250 issued (REF#3480).

197?–Pooch Local Post, Los Gatos, CA
1   **perf**   **L1340**

There is very little information on this local from Los Gatos, Calif., in (probably) the mid-1970s. The stamp design is of a dog's head (of course!) inscribed on the borders with, "POOCH LOCAL POST LOS GATOS CALIF 95030" (REF#8440v4#10/70).

1970–Good Shepard Local Post, Buffalo, New York.
8   **imperf**   **L1360**

In 1970, this Buffalo, N.Y., service issued a design of a cross with a border inscription, "GOOD SHEPHERD LOCAL POST," in red or black printing on seven colors of paper for a total of eight variations (REF#1292).

1971–Estes Park Local Post, Colorado
1   **imperf**   **L1380**

In 1971, this Colorado-based service issued a triangular stamp with black printing on blue paper of an outline drawing of a house and tree. The border is inscribed, "ESTES PARK LOCAL POST ___ ___ " (two words are missing); 300 were issued (REF#1292).

1971–Mountain Climb Local Post
1   **imperf**   **L1400**

An issue of 210 in black printing on yellow paper, with the handwritten inscription, "Last 1971 campout MCLP free" and no other design (REF#1292).

1971-1983–Grand Duchy of Barre Local Post
4   imperf   L1420 (photo)

Three triangular items were issued between 1971 and 1975 by this Chicago and then California-based service.

1) In 1971, the design includes "July 16th audrey 4¢," with a border inscription, "GRAND DUCHY OF BARRE LOCAL POST" printed in black on red paper. Only 192 were issued.
2) In 1972, another Audrey stamp was issued with the same border inscription in a 10-cent denomination with black, blue, purple and red printing on a cream paper; 250 issued.
3) A 1975 issue used a design from a Lithuania triangle with a border inscription, "GRAND DUCHY of BARRE POSTAGE 10¢ LOCAL POSTAGE 10¢," in black printing on yellow paper; 504 were issued.

In 1983, the GD of BLP issued a 30-year commemorative for the Shrub Oak Local Post. The border is inscribed, "30th Anniversary of SHRUB OAK LOCAL POST–GRAND DUCHY OF BARRE LOCAL POST," with the design being the entire original Shrub Oak Local triangle (REF#1292; #8440vol. 13/4).

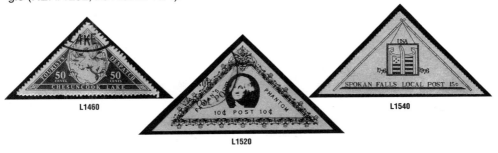

L1460

L1540

L1520

1973–Howard Local Post
2   imperf   L1440

Two items were issued in 1973 inscribed in black, "REPUB. OF MINERVA FOUNDING HOWARD LOCAL POST," each with a 5-cent denomination; 240 of each were issued (REF#1292).

1975–Chesuncook Lake Tourist Local, Chesuncook Village, Maine
6   perf and imperf   L1460 (photo)

In 1975, Chesuncook Village, Maine, issued six stamps to raise money to support its local church. This remote village had no postal service and could only be reached by boat or airplane. These come in three colors and denominations–15-cent red; 25-cent blue; and 50-cent green in both perf and imperf forms. The border is inscribed, "TOURIST'S DESPATCH CHESUHNCOOK LAKE," with three different designs in a central oval–a deer, grouse and moose (REF#8440v4/7).

1975-1976–Cleveland Zoo, Cleveland, Ohio
6   imperf   L1480

In 1975, the Cleveland Zoo introduced its local post stamps as a fund-raiser for the Zoo. They were an issue of three different triangulars for mailing at special boxes at the zoo. They were given a special cancellation by the zoo and then forwarded into the U.S. Postal system–regular U.S. stamps also had to be on the mail. The denominations and designs were: 3 cents, a giant tortoise; 5 cents, King Penguins; and 10 cents, a husky sled dog. Each design was inscribed with, "CLEVELAND ZOO 1975 Local Post," and a naming of the pictured animal. The stamps were issued in sheets of 20, with each sheet being a single denomination.

A second issue in July 1976 had the same denominations with different designs: 3 cents, an American alligator; 10 cents, a bald eagle; and 5 cents, an American bison. They are all inscribed with, "Cleveland Zoological Society 1976 LOCAL POST" (REF#8620Dec. 77/106).

1976-1977–Fabian's Phantom Post
6   imperf   L1520 (photo)

This local post issued six items from early 1976 through mid-1977. They are all inscribed with, "FABIAN'S PHANTOM POST," and all are a 10-cent denomination. Their specifics are:

Vignette	Print color	Paper color
Abe Lincoln	brown	white
G. Washington	brown	white
Tomas Jefferson	brown	white
Ben Franklin	black	gold
An Eagle	red	white
An Eagle	blue	white

1976–Spokan Falls Local Post
1   roulette   L1540 (photo)

A commemorative issue of 325 stamps were done for the USA's bicentennial. Vignette is printed in red on white paper. Inscribed with, "USA 1776 1976 SPOKAN FALLS LOCAL POST 15¢."

1981-1982–Colorado Local Post
2   imperf   L1560

One item has a deep red design depicting a rocket silhouette and is inscribed, "COLORADO LOCAL POST ROCKET MAIL," with a 40-cent value. These were produced in sheets of nine items.

The second item is an identical design in purple in a $1 denomination (REF#7840/9; #8440 vol.14/1; #9010).

1984–Lark Local Post, Oshkosh, Wisconsin
2   imperf   L1580 (photo)

This Oshkosh, Wis., service started in 1984 with a single triangular stamp of black printing on blue-green paper inscribed, "5¢ LARK LOCAL POST OSHKOSH, WI FAST–COURTEOUS" (REF#8440 vol.19/4).

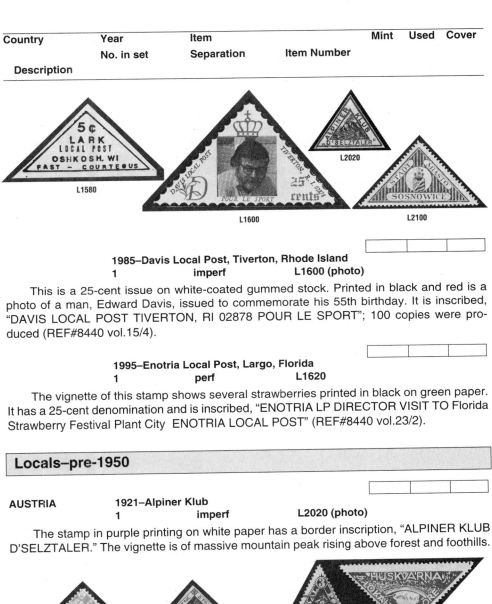

1985–Davis Local Post, Tiverton, Rhode Island
1   imperf   L1600 (photo)

This is a 25-cent issue on white-coated gummed stock. Printed in black and red is a photo of a man, Edward Davis, issued to commemorate his 55th birthday. It is inscribed, "DAVIS LOCAL POST TIVERTON, RI 02878 POUR LE SPORT"; 100 copies were produced (REF#8440 vol.15/4).

1995–Enotria Local Post, Largo, Florida
1   perf   L1620

The vignette of this stamp shows several strawberries printed in black on green paper. It has a 25-cent denomination and is inscribed, "ENOTRIA LP DIRECTOR VISIT TO Florida Strawberry Festival Plant City ENOTRIA LOCAL POST" (REF#8440 vol.23/2).

Locals–pre-1950

AUSTRIA   **1921–Alpiner Klub**
      1   imperf   L2020 (photo)

The stamp in purple printing on white paper has a border inscription, "ALPINER KLUB D'SELZTALER." The vignette is of massive mountain peak rising above forest and foothills.

CZECHOSLOVAKIA **1867–Express Compagnie**
      11   imperf   L2040

This was a local delivery company in Leitmeritz. Its 25 Kreuzer stamp is triangular with a border inscription, "LEITMERITZ ED. HOFER EXPRESS-COMPAGNIE," around a central area with a large "25" in it. These were printed on 11 different color papers: brown, chamois, dark blue, dark green, gray, light blue, light green, lilac, orange, rose and yellow (REF#441/151; #4605/122).

GERMANY

Pre-1900—six different local post services

29   perf and imperf   L2060 (photo)

Germany had a very large number of private mail services in the 25 years preceding 1900. Six of these services issued triangular stamps. These triangular items represent a very small portion of the local post stamps issued. For example, in Frankfurt, there were 158 locals issued during this period, with only 10 of those being triangular—and that is a higher than typical proportion.

Bergedorf-1887—One triangular item was issued depicting a peasant woman and a harvest gathered in baskets. The central vignette is printed in green on white paper with an orange border inscribed, "Brief.Beförd.Ges. 2 Pfennig BERGEDORF." It is perforated.

Berlin-1891—This perforated item was issued by a stenographic service, probably for their use in delivering work they did. The vignette is of a seated figure. The border contains shorthand notation on two sides and "BERLIN" on the base. It is printed in pale brown and emerald green.

Frankfurt -1887—An extensive set of triangulars was issued by this local service. There are 10 denominations in both perf and imperf forms. The vignette depicts a statue of an un-clothed woman sitting on a draped cloth astride a lion. The border inscription is, "FRANK-FURT aM 5 FRIEDENSSTR. 5 PRIVAT- CIRCULAR-POST." The stamp's denomination is indicated on the base of the statue, like "3 PFENNIG 3." Each denomination is printed in a different color on white paper as follows:

Denomination	Color
1pf	blue
2pf	green
3pf	red
5pf	yellow
10pf	pink
20pf	brown
50pf	lilac
1m	copper
5m	silver
10m	gold

Hamburg-1888—A perforated item printed in red and green with a vignette of a big "5" and a border inscription, "STADTBRIEFBEF. zu HAMBURG NACHPORTO." "STADT-BRIEFBEF." is a contraction of "STADTBRIEFBEFORDERUNG," which means "convey-ance of letter mail in a town." Glasewald indicates this is a postage-due item.

Koln-1889—Two perforated items were produced by this delivery service. The design, the same on each, is of a head wearing a winged cap, possibly representing Mercury, the winged messenger of the Gods. The border inscription is, "INTERN. BRIEF & CIRCULAR VERKEHR KOLN," with the denomination in each lower corner. The 1 pfennig is in blue, and the 2 pfennig in red.

Stuttgart -1888—Four imperf items were issued with their vignette being a "3" inside a circular ring. The border is inscribed, "PRIVAT-STADT POST, STUTTGART." They were all for a 3-pfennig denomination. The four colors used, one per item, are brown, dark green, ultramarine and red.

(REF#1760/11,13,62,82,103,143; #8740 July68/643)

Country	Year	Item		Mint	Used	Cover
	No. in set	Separation	Item Number			
Description						

1945–Grossraeschen
1   perf   L2080

During the occupation of Grossraeschen, Germany from July 1945 through October 1946, there was a shortage of stamps, so the post office used its triangular COD label as a regular postage stamp. It hand wrote the denominations and crossed out the "Rembourse-ment" (REF#1570; #3886).

POLAND   1916–Sosnowice
1   perf   L2100 (photo)

Sosnowice issued a local printed in red on white paper. The vignette is of a heraldic shield in a central circle surrounded by a vertical background of alternating red and white stripes. The border text is, "STADT MIASTO SOSNOWICE." Although the stamp does not have a denomination printed on it, it sold for 3 kopecks. This stamp was in use for a two-year period, with 21,600 being issued (REF#500/129; #1990).

SIAM   1883–Ratchaguman locals
4   imperf   L2120

These are attributed to be local issues of a school inside the Royal Palace. One source refers to it as the Peechagumam School, while the other source refers to it as the Rajakumar (royal children) School. Thus, these may have been issued for use inside the palace. The design appears to be a tall temple. All four items are the same except for colors–black on blue green, mauve on cream, black on red, and black on gray (REF#500/126; #1640).

SWEDEN   1888-1945–Six different local post services
27   perf and some imperf   L2140 (photo)

Sweden has had various local posts that have issued triangular items.

Goteborg-1888–A 5-ore stamp was issued in blue with a central vignette of standing in-tertwined figures that have the appearance of a classical sculpture. The border is inscribed, "LOKAL POST GOTEBORG." The denomination appears in all three corners of the border. Although the issue was perforated for the public's use, imperf copies were used on the Loka-post's own mail. Later the same year, a 3-ore perforated stamp in dark ultramarine was issued with the same design as the above item. However, 1,000 copies were issued imperf. A few months later, it issued another perforated stamp printed in yellow, but with no denomination–instead of a number it had stars in the three corners. A year later, it issued the same item with a hand-stamped surcharge of 1 ore, 2 ore, or 10 ore in violet or blue-violet. This local post was very enterprising–it even issued its own postal stationery. In 1888, it produced three different envelopes with the postage (stamp) printed on the envelope. The printed stamp design is the same as its actual stamp. In 1889, Goteborg issued four different postcards with the stamp printed on the card. Again, the printed stamp design is the same as its actual stamp.

Huskvarna-1945–This Swedish town of 10,000 people had a local post that issued two attractive triangulars. The design is an apex downward vignette of the Huskvarna Falls as seen through the Adalen Bridge. Although there is not an explicit border, there is wording around the edges oriented toward reading easily from the designed position, which helps increase its attractiveness. The wording is, "HUSKVARNA LOKALT 50 ORE" or "70 ORE." The 50-ore stamp is in carmine, and the 70-ore in ultramarine, both on white paper. They were produced in sheets of eight, with two connected blocks of four, each with the apexes meeting in the center of the block.

Jönköping-1945–The Huskvarna triangles were overprinted with "Jönköping" for use in that city.

Kalmar-1945–Again the Huskvarna triangles were overprinted, but this time for use in Kalmar.

Stockholm-1925–In 1925, the non-denominated yellow Goteborg local stamp from 35 years earlier was used for a local service in Stockholm, run by the organizer of the earlier Goteborg local. The stamps were overprinted with either "Stockholm" or "STOCKHOLM" in black or violet.

Tranås-1945–Again the Huskvarna triangles were overprinted, but this time for use in Tranås.

(REF#464/133; #500/59,132; #5560/471-486)

USA   **1887–Richwood's Dispatch, Iowa**
          1   imperf   L2160

In La Hoyt, Iowa, in 1887, a local carrier service issued a triangular item. Printed in red on white paper, it shows a portrait of James C. Jay, creator of the carrier service, a denomination of "1," and a border with the inscription, "RICHWOOD'S DISPATCH. PAID TO THE POST OFFICE." The service accepted mail, taking it three miles from the rural area of Richwoods to the La Hoyt post office, and delivering items back to "regular" customers (REF#3220).

Locals–postal strike

On the rare occasions when a governmental postal service goes on strike, there are businessmen ready to step into the void and establish alternative delivery services. These services invariably use stamps to pre-pay their deliveries.

GREAT BRITAIN   **1971**

The 1971 British postal strike lasted for seven weeks, and there were many services established during that time. A few of these services used the triangular format.

          1971–Bexhill Delivery
          1   imperf   L3020

In February 1971, the Bexhill Delivery Service issued a green and white 5-pence stamp with its name inscribed on the three borders. The central design is a letter "A" on top of a letter "S" in a style similar to the comic-book Superman emblem. These were for mail delivery in the local Bexhill area (REF#4672/17).

L3040

OA1020

L4020

OA1040

Country	Year	Item		Mint	Used	Cover
	No. in set	Separation	Item Number			
Description						

1971–City of London Delivery
10　　　　roulette with imperf **L3040 (photo)**

This service covered the city and its stamps depict a coat of arms and are inscribed with, "1971 CITY OF LONDON DELIVERY." The city issued sheets of stamps rouletted both horizontally and vertically. Each "square" contained two triangular stamps joined imperf. Thus, they could be used as a pair, or cut apart for the lowest postal rate. It initially issued larger stamps in 1/ and 2/ denominations printed in black on either pink or yellow paper. Two weeks later, it issued smaller items in 5p and 10p denominations printed in mauve on the same pink and yellow paper.

The above is according to Rosen. However, I also have a set of large size 1/-5p printed in black on the pink and yellow papers. (Were other denominations printed later in the smaller size?) (REF#4672/21)

1971–East Anglican Weekly
5　　　　imperf　　　　**L3060**

There were five denominations issued for this service that covered all of the United Kingdom on a weekly basis, my assumption based upon the company's name. The issues are 2 1/2 pence black, 5p green, 10p blue, 15p red and 25p brown (REF#4672/26).

1971–Emergency Mail
2　　　　imperf　　　　**L3080**

These items have black printing on white paper with a date of 1964 on both. One has a border inscription, "EMERGENCY MAIL G.P.O. STRIKE weight lbs ozs," with the outline of a Mini-Minor with 1964 on the door and a center inscription of "6d S.W.1" (the denomination and the area of London covered). The other is a 2s denomination with the outline of a Volkswagen (REF#7060/14).

1971–Herm Island
?　　　　probably perf　　　　**L3100**

It has been reported the 1957 triangular Herm Island set was overprinted with "1971 STRIKE POST." Apparently it also exists with inverted overprints.

Locals–railway

Railway stamps were used when a railway line expedited the delivery of a letter or parcel. They often were used in conjunction with the normal postage. The item would be "mailed" at the local train station and taken by rail to the city of its destination, where the regular postal service was used to do the delivery.

FINLAND　　　**1878-1903**
13　　　　some perf,
　　　　　　　some imperf　　　　**L4020 (photo)**

A series of similar size and style triangular stamps were used in Finland over a 35-year period for railway delivery of mail. The style is of a large printed numeral; the denomination with either "PENNI" or "MARK." The bottom inscription is "BORGÅ-KERVO BANAN," until 1893 when it became, "BORGÅ JERNVÅG." Specifics on these items are as follows:

Year	Denomination	Paper color	Print Color	Separation
1878	25	dark lilac	black	perf
1878	50	dark lilac	black	perf
1884	50	blue	black	perf
1884	70	chamois	black	perf
1888	30	?	blue	perf
1888	40	?	orange	perf
1888	50	red lilac	black	perf
1888	1 markka	?	black	perf
1893	25	?	blue	perf
1898	25	?	red	imperf
1903	25	?	dark red	imperf
1903	25	?	light red	imperf
1903	25	?	salmon pink	imperf

Note: The denomination is in penniä, unless otherwise indicated. Also, the 1898 item has "seven sun rays" in the design, whereas the 1903 item has "five sun rays." (REF#2043/88; #2064/86)

Other airmail–essay and semi-official

CUBA   **1935–Columbus specimen issue**
      4   perf   OA1020 (photo)

These four items were prepared by the "Colombian Society," as in Christopher Columbus, but they were never issued. There are four denominations with two designs. They were overprinted "MUESTRA" in either red or black. Specifically:

Denomination	Color	Design	Overprint color
5c	violet	d1	red
10c	black brown	d2	red
20c	carmine	d1	black
50c	blue	d2	red

Design "d1" is of two men in old-time attire conversing outside a rectangular-shaped building with a double-engine plane flying overhead; "d2" is of Columbus' three ships sailing on the ocean, with a single-engine plane flying overhead–the apex is down on this design. The inscription on both is, "REPUBLICA de CUBA CORREO AEREO" (REF#4740/919).

ECUADOR   **1939–airmail**
      5   perf   OA1040 (photo)

These five items were to have been used as airmail stamps by Ecuador. They were produced by the Ecuador Columbus Society to honor Columbus. The society was to get part of the proceeds from its sale. Due to public objections, the deal was canceled. However, four years later the society sold them directly to collectors.

The stamps all have the same design–a single engine flying boat in front of a globular map of North and South America, plus one of Columbus' ships sailing in the lower right corner. The lower border is inscribed, "REPUBLICA DEL ECUADOR SERVICIO AEREO," with a "1936" appearing on the lower part of the globe. The stamps were then overprinted in red or black with a denomination and "1939." The stamps are each in a single color that differs for each denomination–5 ctvs is blue; 10 ctvs is brown; 50 ctvs is light green; 1 sucre is red; and 5 sucres is dark green

OA1060   OA1100   OA1120

FRANCE   **1924–Vincennes Aviation Meeting**
          8   perf   OA1060 (photo)

These items were issued for use on mail carried at an aviation meeting with a flight from Vincennes to Le Bourget. The vignette is a biplane flying with some buildings in the right hand background. The inscription is, "POSTE PAR AVION VINCENNES," and the date "9 Juin 1924." All have the same design and are on white paper.

Denomination	Border color	Accent color
25c	mauve	red
50c	red	brown
75c	green	blue
1Fr	lilac	blue
2Fr	yellow	gray
5Fr	blue	brown
25c surcharge on 50c	red	brown
25c surcharge on 75c	green	blue

(REF#4740/268)

PARAGUAY   **1929–Essay**
          4   imperf   OA1080

These four items, with a 4.75 peso denomination, are one design in four different colors--blue, brown on yellow, green and yellow. The vignette is of an airplane flying over a jungle of palm trees with the sun in the background. The two side borders are inscribed, "SERVICO AEROPOSTAL REPUBLICA DEL PARAGUAY" (REF#4740/902).

PUERTO RICO   **1940–Second Aerovias Issue**
          8   perf   OA1100 (photo)

In 1940, a set of private airmail stamps was issued by Aerovias Nacionales Puerto Rico Inc. for use on mail carried on routes of the airline in the Caribbean. These were issued and used with the full approval of the government. Eight denominations were issued in miniature sheets of six stamps of the same value. The design, inscriptions in black, and a gray background, are the same for all denominations, while the accent color differs. The design is of the Statue of Liberty on the left side, a flying two-engine airplane in the center, the New York World's Fair pylon and sphere on the right side, and the denomination in the two lower corners—all this is in the accent color. The inscription is, "PORTE AEREO AEROVIAS PUERTO RICO INC," with an outline map of an island inscribed "PUERTO RICO."

Denomination	Accent color	Quantity issued
1c	blue green	10,000
3c	red violet	10,000
5c	blue	10,000
10c	yellow	10,000
15c s.charge in black on $1	brown	4,500
25c	green	6,000
50c	purple	6,000
$1	brown	1,500

For another viewpoint on how "legitimate" these items might have been, there is a very interesting letter on the subject published in REF#7300 Aug. 15, 1994. This letter raises the possibility they were issued as "a money-making and publicity stunt" (REF#4740/668; #7300 Aug. 15, 1994).

SWITZERLAND   **1925–International Aviation Meeting**
         8   **perf and imperf**   **OA1120 (photo)**

These items were used for a special flight from Geneva to Paris to Geneva to Basel. There are four items that come in both perf and imperf. These four are all the same design and bordering, except two are inscribed with "SUISSE-FRANCE" and two with "SUISSE-EUROPE CENTRALE." The vignette is of three flying planes with the large center one being a biplane. The rest of the inscription is, "MEETING INTERNATIONAL SERVICE AERIEN." The border printing is in ultramarine. There were 5,000 issued of each.

Type	Papercolor	Vignette and denomination color
SUISSE-FRANCE 30c	white	red
SUISSE-FRANCE 50c	white	green
SUISSE-EUROPE CENTRALE 30c	yellow	red
SUISSE-EUROPE CENTRALE 50c	greenish	green

(REF#4740/800)

        1927–Brugg
         1   **perf**   **OA1140**

This was a very limited issue of 450 items for a special flight from Brugg to Yverdon. These black and blue items have a line drawing of a stylized bird carrying an envelope with the words, "FLVG POST," underneath. There is a border inscription, "DESTALOZZI GEDENKFEIER BRUGG 1927" (REF#444/204; #4740/802).

UNKNOWN   **19??–European Air Service?**
        15   **perf**   **OA1160 (photo)**

Five countries were going to participate in a common air-carrier plan (whose?). There is a separate design for each country. From the style and design of the stamps it looks as if this was created in the late 1920s (exactly when?). There is no denomination on the stamps. These items were issued as a sheetlet of 10 stamps in the five designs, with one to four copies of each design. Purple and red-orange and at least one other color exist. (How many colors were used?) Each sheetlet is printed in only one color on white paper.

Inscription	Possible country	Quantity in sheet	Design
PAR AVION	France	4	Single engine biplane over birds, open space, and a few buildings.
POSTA AEREA	Italy	1	Single engine biplane over lots of big buildings including factories.
BY AIR MAIL	USA	2	A strange looking single wing, three-body airplane flying over the Statue of Liberty.
MIT FLUGPOST	Germany	2	A bi-wing flying boat is flying over industrial plants.
CU AVION	?Romania?	1	A bi-wing plane is flying over a river and bridge.

OA1160

Other airmail–pigeon post

NEW ZEALAND   1899–pigeongram
                  2   perf   OA2020 (photo)

In 1894, the SS Wairarapa ran aground on the Great Barrier island with the loss of 135 lives. The lack of a way to let others know about events on Great Barrier led to the use of pigeons to carry messages and mail from Great Barrier to Auckland.

These are the world's first triangular air-mail stamps. They were produced and used from 1899-1908 to convey messages to and from the Great Barrier Island and Auckland, 65 miles away. The stamp was used both to signify that the proper postage had been paid, and to secure the message paper into a small enough package to go on a pigeon's leg. It has been reported that the triangular design resulted from the desire of the New Zealand postal authorities to have these stamps be readily distinguishable from regular postal stamps (REF#9110/204).

Both stamps are of the same design–a flying carrier pigeon in a circle surrounded by a lacy design. The border is inscribed, "GREAT BARRIER ISLd PIGEON-GRAM AUCKLAND." The 6-d blue stamps were produced in sheets of 20, and 10,000 were issued. The red 1sh was produced in strips of 10, with 5,000 being issued. The 6d were used for flights from Auckland to the island, and the 1sh were used for flights from the island to Auckland.

Imperf proof copies of these items exist (REF#447/171; #2430/73; #8410/161; #8980/204).

Also, see the New Zealand items in the Postage Stamp listing and in the "Philatelica–Commemmorative" section.

OA2020   OA3020   OA3040   OA3060

Other airmail–rocket mail

In the early 1930s, there was experimentation in many countries with using rockets as a means for delivering mail. Postage stamps were sold for use on the letters carried by the rockets as a way for raising money to help finance the experiments.

Many of these early stamps were made triangular in design and shape. A general reference is REF#7165. REF#1360, the Ellington Zwisler Rocket Mail Catalogue, has its own numbering scheme. Those reference numbers are indicated herein as "EZ --" followed by their identifier.

AUSTRALIA 1935–Fraser Island - SS Maheno
2 imperf OA3020 (photo)

An experimental two-way mail-delivery system using rockets was tried between Fraser Island and the SS Maheno, a Japanese ship wreck off Fraser Island. The Queensland Airmail Society prepared 3,000 stamps in sheets of four for each direction of the flights. The red triangle was used for the shore-to-ship flight, and a green triangle for the ship-to-shore flight. The vignette is of a two masted, two funnel ship off a coast with a rocket flying inland. The border inscription reads, "MAHENO-FRASER ISLAND WRECK ROCKET FLIGHT AUSTRALIA." EZ–2A1,3A1

References for the above item and the four below include (REF#1360/1-5; #2430/29-31; #7150/205)

1936–RT6
1 imperf OA3040 (photo)

The Australian Rocket Society issued 1,600 stamps in sheets of four to use for an experiment across the Moggill River. This triangle, with its apex down, is in orange brown. Its vignette has a central triangle surrounding a line drawing of a rocket with large letters "R T 6" in the three corners inside the outer border. The border is inscribed, "AUSTRALIA ROCKET FIRING." EZ–6A1

1936–RT7
1 imperf OA3060 (photo)

The Australian Rocket Society issued 1,600 stamps in sheets of four to use for an experiment at the Engorra Rifle Range in Brisbane. This triangle, with its apex down, is in green with a vignette of a flying rocket and large letters "R T 7" in the three border corners. The border is inscribed, "AUSTRALIA YOUNG·ROCKET EXPERIMENT." EZ–7A1

1937–RO3
1 imperf OA3080 (photo)

The Australian Rocket Society issued 1,600 stamps in sheets of four to use for an experiment at Camp Mountain in Brisbane. This triangle, with its apex up, is in blue with a vignette of a rocket flying over the earth and large letters "R O 3" in the three border corners. The border is inscribed, "YOUNG ROCKET EXPERIMENT AUSTRALIA." EZ–9A1

1937–RZ2
1 imperf OA3100 (photo)

Country	Year	Item		Mint	Used	Cover
	No. in set	Separation	Item Number			
Description						

The Australian Rocket Society issued 1,600 stamps in sheets of four to use for an experiment at the Engorra Rifle Range in Brisbane. This triangle, with its apex up, is in brown. Its vignette is of a rocket over mountains being lowered by parachute after its flight. There are large letters "R Z 2" in the three border corners. The border is inscribed, "YOUNG ROCKET EXPERIMENT AUSTRALIA." EZ–10A1

OA3100

OA3140

OA3180

AUSTRIA   **1928–Stratosphere Flight Stamp**
          3   imperf   OA3120

This issue was for Stratosphere Balloon flight(s), which attempted to launch a rocket from a high altitude reached by the balloon, thus getting more distance from the rocket's fuel. The vignette is of a balloon with a square gondola in one stamp, and with a triangular gondola in the other. They were printed on tissue paper in orange and black with 100 of each issued. These were printed se-tenant. The border is inscribed, "3 Groschen F.S.1 16000-18000m Hochflugpost." The third stamp, of which only 25 copies were produced, is the triangular gondola stamp with a small rocket in flight above the balloon. EZ–1A1,1A2,1A3 (REF#1360/6; #3090/25; #7615/270)

          1932-1933–Raketenflugpost
          5   mixed   OA3140 (photo)

These five triangular rocket-mail stamps all have the same design–an airborne rocket above land with a background of clouds. They also include the denomination boldly printed on the right-hand side of the design. The bottom inscription says, "RAKETENFLUGPOST IN OESTERREICH." Where paper color is not mentioned, it is white. Item 15A1 is perf, all the rest are imperf. Item 18A1 was printed in sheets of eight stamps.

Year	Denomination	Color	Quantity issued	Reference item
1932	1 schilling	Blue	269	15A1
1933	1 schilling	Blue on spotted light blue paper	960	18A1
1933	60 groschen	Dark green on spotted blue paper	640	20A1
1933	30 groschen	Dark green on spotted blue paper	638	20A2
1933	30 groschen	Purple, with black overprint "Katapultflug"	393	24A1

(REF#1360/13; #3090/27; #8950/365)

BELGIUM   **1935–Duinbergen**
          1   imperf   OA3160

One of a set of three rocket stamps is a triangular. It is printed in canary yellow on white paper. The vignette depicts a launching tube, a rocket flying over a landscape, and clouds in the background. The border is inscribed, "er VOL PAR FUSSEE ste RAKETTENVLUCHT HEYST A/ZEE DUINBERGEN" (REF#4505/1.4.01).

Country	Year	Item		Mint	Used	Cover
Description	No. in set	Separation	Item Number			

1961–Bullange
2   perf and imperf   OA3180 (photo)

These colorful items in red and orange and blue show three rockets, each inscribed "EUROPA," as the stamp's border. The corners have the letters "U B E." The inside is inscribed, "NEDERLAND BELGIQUE DEUTSCHLAND." They were produced in both perf and imperf in sheets of 3. EZ–18A1 (REF#1360/33)

FRANCE   **1935–Sangatte**
1   perf   OA3200

The vignette, in gray, is a graphical stylized rocket with fins in front of a stylized background. The inscription is, "1er VOL PAR FUSEE SANGATTE·1935." These were probably produced in sheets of four labels. This item is not in REF#1360 nor #5990. However, REF#4116 does contain a brief reference to it, including an illustration (REF#4116/101).

GERMANY   **1960–Schifferstadt**
2   imperf   OA3220

These items, one in red, one in blue, are inscribed with, "NRS 626 okt 1960 RAKETV-LUCHT." EZ–21A1, 21A2 (REF#1360/55)

1961–Augsburg
2   imperf   OA3240 (photo)

One item is black printing on pink paper, and the other is black printing on blue paper, inscribed with, "2. (or 3.) VERSUCHSREIHE RAKETEN.VEREIN eV.AUGSBURG." EZ–37A1, 37A2 (REF#1360/63)

OA3240   OA3260   OA3320

GREAT BRITAIN   **1934–London**
6   imperf   OA3260 (photo)

There were six items prepared for use on the first rocket flights in England by Gerald Zucker. Due to technical difficulties, these flights never happened, so these items have been regarded as essays since they weren't used. There are two distinctively different designs.

The first design, D1, in the table below, depicts a man riding on a flying rocket with the label "GOLIGHTLY." Above the rocket is a circle with the denomination. Its border inscription says. "ROCKETFLIGHT LONDON APEX 7-12 MAY 1934."

The second design, D2, depicts a large bulbous flying rocket over land labeled, "NEDERLAND." The stamp was originally prepared for use in Holland. However, the supply of the Golightly stamps ran out in England, so these were surcharged with the English denomination and overprinted with, "ROCKET POST in ENGLAND" or "ROCKET MAIL in ENGLAND"

and sold for the English flight. The border inscription is "VOOR RAKETENVLUCHTEN EN NEDERLAND 1934." All were on white paper unless otherwise indicated below.

Design	Denomination	Color	Quantity issued	EZ number
D1	5 schilling	orange (or vermilion)	1,000	1B1
D1	5 schilling	maroon (or mauve)	500	1B2
D1	prior item surcharged 2/6	maroon (or mauve)	1,350	1B3
D2	50ct, no surcharge	black		1B4
D2	brown surcharge "5 sh"	black	750	1B5
D2	brown surcharge "2/6 sh"	black on yellow paper	900	1B6

(REF#1360/84; #3090/20; #5090/50; #8945/413)

HOLLAND   **1934–not used**
        4   **perf and imperf**   **OA3280**

Although the stamps were prepared and sold, the flights were banned by the Dutch government. One item is a 50ct in light green on white paper showing a flying rocket with a background of (?). It is inscribed, "NEDERLANDSCHE (something) ONDERNEMING RAKETTENPOST." The second item is in blue on white paper with a 1- florin denomination and (probably) the same inscription and a similar vignette. Both items come in perf and imperf forms. They were produced in sheets of four, but there is no reference on the quantities produced. EZ–0A1, 0A3 (REF#1360/99).

        1935–not used
        1   **imperf**   **OA3300**

This item is in blue on white paper showing a rocket in clouds. It is inscribed, "NEDERLAND SE RAKETTENVLUCHT 19·NRB·35." There is no reference on the quantities produced. EZ–0A5 (REF#1360/99).

        1935–Katwijk aan Zee (RV1 and RV2)
        5   **perf and imperf**   **OA3320 (photo)**

These items show a winged rocket in flight and are inscribed, "RAKETENVLIEGTUIG PROEF IN NEDERLAND 1935 · NRB." Two different designs were used. They have no denomination.

Color	Separation	Quantity issued	EZ number
purple	perf and imperf	740	9A1,9A1a
gray	imperf		9A1c
brown	perf and imperf	764	10A1,10A1a

(REF#1360/104)

        1937
        1   **perf**   **OA3340**

This item depicts a rocket in flight and is inscribed, "NEDERLANDSCHE RAKETVLUCHT 1937." The reference has an illustration of this item on cover (REF#7165 Sep. 1994/384).

1938–Feyenoord (SF 2)
1   perf   OA3360

This item is a yellow triangle with some inscription. EZ–24A1 (REF#1360/109).

1945–Amsterdam
3   perf and imperf   OA3380 (photo)

The design is of a rocket flying above a partial globe with the inscription, "RAKET PROEF VLUCHT IN NEDERLAND 1945 ORGANISATIE BRUNO AMSTERDAM."

Color	Separation	EZ number
red	imperf	32A1
red	perf	33A1
purple	perf	35A1

These items were used for eight different flights from four different cities over a three-month period (REF#1360/112; #7165 Sept. 1994/384).

1962–Egmond
2   imperf   OA3400

These issues, one in red and one in blue, have a design of seven rockets radiating outward from a central point and are inscribed, "1962 RAKET POST." The border is a design made from many small triangles. EZ–91A1, 91A2 (REF#1360/138).

OA3380   OA3420   OA3460   OA3540

1965–Zandvoort
3   imperf   OA3420 (photo)

These issues, one in blue, one in green and one in red, depict a rocket in flight above flat ground and are inscribed with large letters, "NRS." EZ–102A1, 102A2, 102A3 (REF#1360/143).

ICELAND   **1970–Reykjavik**
1   imperf   OA3440

In blue printing on white paper the design depicts a polar bear on an ice flow looking up at a plane flying overhead. (This design is identical to the Arctic Air Mercy item listed in the Phantom and Bogus section.) The stamp is inscribed on all three borders, with the bottom inscription being "ISLAND." Only 250 were issued. They were made in sheets of two. EZ–1A1 (REF#5990/347).

ITALY   **1934–Trieste**
       2   imperf   OA3460 (photo)

The 5 Lire red and green, and a 7.70 Lire gray (blue) and green items depict a rocket in flight over the earth as seen from space. They are inscribed, "ESPERIMENTI DI POSTA PER RAZZOESPRESSO TRIESTE OTTOBRE 1934." Four thousand of each were printed in sheets of four. EZ–1A1, 1A2 (REF#1360/178; #5090/84).

      1947 to 1951–San Remo
       2   perf   OA3480

These red (2A1) and red and blue (7A1) printed items have a design of a flying rocket with the border inscribed, "ESPERIMENTO POSTERASZZO SANREMO BORDIGHERA." These may have been produced in sheets of eight. EZ–2A1, 7A1 (REF#1360/178, 181).

YUGOSLAVIA   **1961–Maribor**
       1   ?   OA3500

A plain red triangle with no inscription or other printing. EZ–6A2 (REF#1360/187).

LIECHTENSTEIN   **1935**
       3   imperf   OA3520

The design is a rocket in flight above a background of ground and sky inscribed, "ERSTE RAKCTEN FLUG VADUZ TRIESENBURG." There is a "19" in the lower left corner and a "35" in the lower right corner. These items are in the following colors: brown on pink, olive on white, and blue on white. This item may be an essay since there are no records of any flights. EZ–1A1, 1A1a, 1A1b (REF#1360/192).

LUXEMBOURG   **1962–Rumelange**
       2   perf and imperf   OA3540 (photo)

The design is a red rocket in front of a brown clipper sailing ship inscribed, "Dr.A.J.de-BRUIJN RAKET POST NEDERLAND." These were produced in sheets of four. EZ–6A1,6A1a (REF#1360/195; #7165 Sept. 1994/383).

USA   **1936–NYPE rocket post**
       2   ?   OA3560 (photo)

The New York Philatelic Exhibition of May 1936 issued two small triangular labels showing a rocket in flight over New York City. The 50-cent item of a rocket in flight over New York City has an orange center on white with blue inscriptions. There is also a 75-cent item in the same design with a blue center and orange inscriptions. These are essay items since there were no rocket flights and they were never used in carrying mail. EZ–9A1 (REF#5660/39; #9010 has illustration).

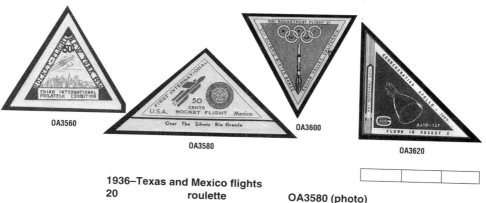

OA3560

OA3580

OA3600

OA3620

1936–Texas and Mexico flights
20   roulette   OA3580 (photo)

The American Legion Post in McAllen, Texas, sponsored a series of 10 rocket flights which carried mail. The flights went between McAllen and Raynosa, Mexico, thus making these the first International Rocket Air Mail Flights. Triangular stamps were sold to raise funds.

All stamps have the same design–a rocket and an American Legion emblem. They are inscribed, "FIRST INTERNATIONAL ROCKET FLIGHT 50 CENTS U.S.A. Mexico." There was a sheet of four printed in red and blue each with different base inscriptions. There was also a sheet of four printed in red and green, again each with different base inscriptions. There were a 1,000 of each of these eight stamps issued.

According to REF#1360, there were also three versions of the USA to Mexico stamp that were overprinted in red with "Trial Flight Experimental Rocket No 1" or "2" or "3." These three versions were used about a month before the official flights. Since there are four different stamps in a sheet, and three different overprints possible, there are 12 different items in this grouping. About 248 stamps were issued with the overprinting. EZ–10A1, 10A2, 10A3, 11A1, 12A1 (REF#1360/216; #7645/64).

1960–Squaw Valley, California
1   imperf   OA3600 (photo)

This item is a blue triangle depicting a rocket and the Olympic Game rings inscribed, "RRI ROCKETPOST FLIGHT VI, VIII OLYMPIC WINTER GAMES SQUAW VALLEY CALIFORNIA." There is also a souvenir sheet with four stamps. EZ–29A1 (REF#1360/226).

1968–Pyramid Lake
3   imperf   OA3620 (photo)

These have a red design inscribed, "RRI ROCKETPOST XVII COMMERMORATING APOLLO 1968 FLOWN IN ROCKET 1 (OR 2 OR 3)." There were 2,200 souvenir sheets issued containing the three stamps. EZ–110A1, 110A2, 110A3 (REF#5990/388).

1968–Pyramid Lake
3   imperf   OA3640

Printed in blue, the vignettes of these items depict each of the three different rocket motors used in an Apollo flight. They are inscribed, "RRI ROCKETPOST XXII COMMERM-

Country	Year	Item		Mint	Used	Cover
	No. in set	Separation	Item Number			
Description						

ORATING APOLLO 8 FLOWN IN ROCKET 1." There were 1,500 souvenir sheets issued containing three triangulars and one other stamp. EZ–112A2, 112A3, 112A4 (REF#5990/389).

Phantoms and bogus

This category of Cinderellas consists of items based on some non-existent reality. Phantoms are stamps issued for imaginary places–places that do not really exist. Bogus stamps are those issued for a real place, but by an imaginary or unauthorized postal authority or service.

Sometimes very little of their background is known. The Arabia and Arctic Air Mercy items below are prime examples of this. For both of these items, the background of their issuance is completely unknown–we do not know who issued them, when they were issued, why they were created, nor where they originated. That is part of the genuine allure of collecting Cinderella items–the mystery associated with them (REF#7630/10).

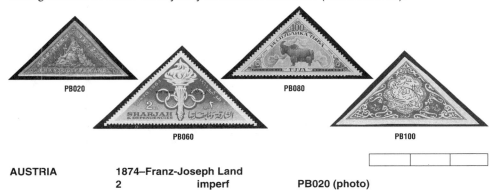

PB020   PB080

PB060   PB100

AUSTRIA   1874–Franz-Joseph Land
2   imperf   PB020 (photo)

These stamps were created by S. Friedl, a Viennese stamp dealer, to commemorate the discovery in 1874 of a group of glaciers by the North Pole Expedition of 1872-74. These two items emulate the Cape of Good Hope design–they depict a woman seated and facing to the left. The central vignette is surrounded by a border reminiscent of the Cape's border. One item, in green, has a border notation, "CAP PEST 1872-74 FRANZ JOSEPH LAND." The other item, in orange, is inscribed, "CAP WIEN 1872-74 FRANZ JOSEPH LAND." Note that the designs on each of these stamps are of different women (REF#470/197; #865/38; #5703/104; #6001/99).

FRANCE   1968–Ile Roy
24   perf and imperf   PB040

Ile Roy is a fictitious "country" used by A. Bouridi for numerous stamps he created. Bouridi is a renown French specialist in Cinderella items and has written several books and journals on Cinderellas.

This issue commemorates the 60th Anniversary of the Sicilian Earthquake of 1908. (See the issues under labels and seals-charity fund-raising for Italy and USA.) These items are a close reproduction of the Italian item's design. Only two design aspects were changed: The name "ILE ROY" replaced the denomination of the original, and the "1908" at the bottom of the original was changed to "1908 1968."

The original Earthquake issue has 11 different designs. It is not clear if Bouridi's items were issued in only a single design of horse-drawn peasant cart or whether more of the 11 designs were also used. Like the original issue, Bouridi's issue comes in different color combinations:

Number of colors used per item	Colors available	Separation	Quantity issued
one	blue-turquoise	perforate	26 sets
	yellow		
	emerald green		
	violet		
	gray		
	red		
one	same as above	imperforate	14 sets
two	gray with blue-turquoise	perforate	50 sets
	violet with yellow		
	red with emerald green		
	blue-turquoise with gray		
	yellow with violet		
	emerald green with red		
two	same as above	imperforate	250 sets

(REF#845/102)

KHOR FAKKAN   **1965**
                  7   **perf and imperf**   **PB060 (photo)**

This small fishing village on the Gulf of Oman in the country of Sharjah "issued" overprints on the 1965 Sharajah triangles. These are bogus stamps since the village had no postal service and produced them only to raise revenue from stamp collectors.

There are two sets of three items, one perforated, the other imperf, with a design based on the Olympic Games. These are the October 1964 triangle set of Sharjah overprinted with "Khor Fakkan". There is also a souvenir sheet with the same overprint, again created from the Sharjah set.

TANNA TUVA   **1994–"postage" stamps**
                  12   **perf and imperf**   **PB080 (photo)**

These modern Tanna Tuvan stamps are six items issued in both perf and imperf forms. The designs are somewhat similar to the sets from the late 1930s in style and subjects. The main inscription, in Russian, is roughly, "PECIIYbₐNKA TbIBA TUVA."

I have classified these as Cinderella and bogus since it is not clear at this time whether they were issued by an authorized governmental agency. Apparently they were printed in Austria, but for whom and how they are distributed is not clear (REF#8395).

UNKNOWN   **1922–Arabia phantom**
               5   **imperf**   **PB100 (photo)**

These items are all of the same vignette, a central "rosette" containing Arabic script with ornate flowing line designs in each of the three corners. The script in the center translates into, "In the name of God, the most compassionate, the most merciful." The items were issued in five different colors, with each color being a different denomination, which are in the lower two corners. The blue is 50 paras, the red is 75 paras, the green 1 piastre, the orange 2 piastre, and the purple 5 piastre (REF#845/14; #7090).

Country	Year	Item		Mint	Used	Cover
	No. in set	Separation	Item Number			
Description						

USA   1934–Atlantis
             7   rouletted   PB120

These stamps are attributed to a Captain Mott in Miami. For what purpose is a subject for speculation. See REF#7570 for an interesting account related to these, and other, stamps of Atlantis.

These seven depict a crest of Neptune–a crown, spread wings, a portrait of Neptune holding a trident within a circular area, and at the bottom a ribbon inscribed, "SERC KREDI VIDI." The name "ATLANTIS" and a denomination also appear. These items are all with the apex at the bottom of the stamp. The denominations and colors are as follows: 2 sk (Skalog) in black on cream paper; 3 sk in black on cream; 7 sk in black on orange; 75 sk (in colors unknown to this author) (REF#845/110; #7420-Jan. 69/14; #7600/12; #7570/10).

             ?–Alaska mercy flight
             40   perf   PB140 (photo)

These items have an ongoing aura of mystery surrounding them. Over the years, various stamp publications have been asked for information on them from readers who have run across one or more. Invariably, the publication confirms that we do not know much about these items.

The items are all the same design, inscription and denomination. The design is of a polar bear standing on an ice floe looking up at an airplane flying overhead. The plane appears to have a single engine and an overhead wing. The inscription is, "ARCTIC AIR MERCY FLIGHT ALASKA." The denomination is a 10 in each lower corner. The printing and perforation used on these items is of a high quality. The gum surface has a distinct texture like grained leather. All the items I have seen are perforated.

There are different combinations of paper, color of border, color of the design's background and overprinting. The paper is either a white (by far the most common) or a very heavy yellow stock. The yellow stock items were probably issued without gum. The overprinting is the addition of a solid gold or silver band on the border area. Below are items issued:

Paper	Border	Background	No overprinting	Gold overprinting	Silver overprinting
White	gray	mauve	x	x	x
White	gray	blue	x	x	x
White	gray	green	x	x	x
White	gray	red	x	x	x
White	gray	orange	x	x	x
White	mauve	red	x	x	x
White	blue	red	x	x	x
White	green	red	x	x	x
White	yellow	red	x	x	x
White	carmine	red	x	x	x
Yellow	mauve	red	x		
Yellow	blue	red	x		
Yellow	green	red	x		
Yellow	yellow	red	x		
Yellow	carmine	red	x		

Country		Year		Item		Mint	Used	Cover
		No. in set		Separation	Item Number			
Description								

Paper	Border	Background	No overprinting	Gold overprinting	Silver overprinting
Yellow	gray	mauve	x		
Yellow	gray	blue	x		
Yellow	gray	green	x		
Yellow	gray	red	x		
Yellow	gray	orange	x		

There are reports of the yellow paper items also having the gold overprinting, but I have not been able to confirm it (REF#7300-Jan. 6, 1992; #8620-March 1981/68).

Philatelica–advertising

CHINA   **1957–Tian Jin promotional labels**
              4   **rough perf**   **P1020 (photo)**

Tian Jin is a large city near Beijing. These items depict a two-engine propeller-driven airplane flying in front of some clouds. They are inscribed, in three rows of Chinese, which translates to, "AIR MAIL IS THE FASTEST-It can reach all places both within and outside the country." The items are made from a poor quality paper, have ragged perforations and come in black, blue, green and red.

GREAT BRITAIN   **? –Barnett-Stamp dealer's publicity label**
                    1   **imperf**   **P1040**

An auction catalog referenced a stamp dealer's publicity label from Barnett, Ilchester in the form of an imitation of the Cape of Good Hope triangle printed in green.

          ?–H.A.Kennedy & Co. - Stamp dealer's publicity label
          1   **unknown**   **P1060**

This New Oxford St. (London) dealer used the Cape of Good Hope design with the company name inscribed in the border (REF#8080/141).

          ?–Berry-Stamp dealer's publicity label
          1   **imperf**   **P1080**

The central vignette of this label is the Cape vignette printed in black on a red background. Border is black with red inscription, "37 MOORFIELDS LIVERPOOL 2 D.A.BERRY (H. SINCLAIR BROWN)."

          ?–Field - Stamp dealer's publicity label
          1   **imperf**   **P1100**

This item's vignette is of two flying planes with the border inscribed, "FRANCIS J. FIELD Ltd SUTTON COLDFIELD EVERYTHING AIRPOST SPECIALISTS." Pale green paper with black printing.

          ?–Stanley Gibbons-"Stamp Weekly"
          1   **imperf**   **P1120**

This advertisement label for Stanley Gibbons Ltd. used the Cape of Good Hope design with a border inscription, "GIBBONS STAMP WEEKLY ONE PENNY" (REF#8080/140).

?–Stanley Gibbons-Monthly Journal
1   **unknown**   **P1140**

This advertisement label for Stanley Gibbons Ltd. used the Cape of Good Hope design but had a border inscription of "MONTHLY JOURNAL 3/- PER ANNUM" (REF#8080/140).

HOLLAND   **?–W. Russell-Stamp dealer's publicity label**
2   **unknown**   **P1160**

A stamp dealer's publicity label with a design imitating the Cape triangle. They are printed in mauve or in purple with the inscription, "W. Russell,Haarlem,Schouwtjesplein 5."

P1020   P1180   P2020   P2060

SWITZERLAND   **?–Ed Estoppey**
1   **imperf**   **P1180 (photo)**

This item is on white paper with dark blue printing. The vignette is a Cape of Good Hope triangle. The border is inscribed, "ED.S.ESTOPPEY TIMBRES pour Collections Galerie St. Francois LAUSANNE." The images and the lettering are in white.

USA   **?–Amer Berolina Co., New York**
1   **unknown**   **P1200**

This New York dealer used the Cape of Good Hope design with the border inscribed, "52 WEST 47TH ST NEW YORK CITY AMERBEROLINA CO" (REF#8080/141).

?–Bombay Philatelic Co., New York
1   **unknown**   **P1220**

This New York dealer used the Cape of Good Hope design with the company name inscribed in the border (REF#8080/141).

Philatelica–commemorative

AUSTRALIA   **1957–Adelaide-Gawler flight**
3   **perf and imperf**   **P2020 (photo)**

This item was made for use on mail carried on a 1957 flight commemorating the 40th anniversary of the first South Australian airmail flight. The vignette is of an airplane, a Bleriot 60, printed in red on a blue background. The border is inscribed in red, "GRAHAM CAREY SPECIAL AIR MAIL 40th ANNIVERSARY OF FIRST AIR MAIL WITHIN STH. AUSTRALIA." These were produced in sheets of four in both perf and imperf forms.

Country	Year	Item		Mint	Used	Cover
	No. in set	Separation	Item Number			
Description						

In 1967, the remaining stamps were overprinted in black with "50th/1967" for use in commemoration of the 50th Anniversary. These items were only produced on the perforated stamps (REF#2430/42).

NEW ZEALAND 1949–Great Barrier Pigeon Post 50th Anniv.
　　　　　　　　　2　　　　　imperf　　　　　P2040

The Air Mail Society of New Zealand issued two commemorative labels for the 50th Anniversary of the Great Barrier Island Agency pigeon mail service. These labels replicate the red and blue 6d and 1sh stamps used by the agency. The replicas are slightly smaller than the originals, they have much poorer quality printing, the colors are much darker than the originals, and they have a golden border. These were produced in souvenir sheets of three of each stamp (six stamps per sheet). (REF#2430/74).

　　　　　　　　　1994–Great Barrier Pigeon Post Commemorative
　　　　　　　　　2　　　　　perf　　　　　P2060 (photo)

Two stamps were issued by the Great Barrier Pigeon-Gram Service in 1994 to commemorate the use of pigeon mail. These two stamps depict a pigeon flying above the SS Wairarapa, a steam ship with one funnel and four sails. The borders are inscribed, "GREAT BARRIER PIGEON POST 29th OCTOBER 1894." The stamps have two denominations: 1/6 and $15.

Philatelica–exhibitions

GREAT BRITAIN 1912–Margate - 4th Phil Congress of Great Britain
　　　　　　　　　12　　　　　roulette, imperf,
　　　　　　　　　　　　　　(perf?)　　　　　P3020 (photo)

Stamps for the Fourth Philatelic Congress of Great Britain were issued in sheets of 18 stamps in nine tete-beche pairs with roulette separations. The central design is of a standing woman with trident, helmet and shield. In the background is a lighthouse, sailing ship and the ocean. The border is inscribed, "FOURTH PHILATELIC CONGRESS of Gt.BRITAIN." There were six different colors of border: blue, brown, green, red, red-brown and violet, with black centers. Also, some sheets were made with black borders and colored centers. There is no denomination on any of them (REF#886/18).

(An auction catalog entry for these items indicated a perforated form. Was this a catalog misprint or were they also issued with perforations?)

P3020　　　　　　　　　　P3040　　　　　　　　　　P3060

SOUTH AFRICA   1928–South African Intl. Stamp Exhibition
9   imperf and roulette P3040 (photo)

These items use the design from the Cape of Good Hope triangles with a border inscribed, "S. AFRICAN INTERNATIONAL STAMP EXHIBITION." There is an added banner underneath the seated figure that reads, "DURBAN JULY 1928." Since each stamp I have seen is inscribed underneath the stamp with "FOR PARTICULARS WRITE TO: P.O. BOX 588, DURBAN, NATAL," I assume they were produced in sheetlets of four items all of the same color. The items I have seen are:

Separation	Paper color	Printing color
Imperforate	dark blue	brown
Imperforate	flesh (salmon)	brown
Imperforate	flesh (salmon)	red-orange
Imperforate	light blue	red-orange
Imperforate	pink	brown
Imperforate	pink	dark green
Imperforate	white	dark green
Imperforate	white	red-orange
Rouletted	orange	dark brown

The number of printing colors, paper colors and separation styles leads to wondering about how many different stamps were created. (Please let me know if you are aware of examples of additional items.) (REF#8080/141)

SWEDEN   1945–Frimarkets dag
4   perf   P3060 (photo)

Sweden's 1945 Official Stamp Day (frimarkets dag) was the occasion for the issuance of this triangular item. The vignette is of a dove flying above the earth with an (olive) branch in its mouth. The inscription is, "1945 FRIMÄRKETS DAG För fatid orh framtid." It was issued in sheetlets of eight in four different colors: blue-violet, green, orange, and red-violet–one color per sheet (REF#7960).

USA   1934–Gloucester Philatelic Society
4   imperf   P3080 (photo)

The Gloucester Philatelic Society, Gloucester, Mass., issued sheets of four imperf stamps with black printing on green, blue, orange and pink papers. The border inscription is, "GLOUCESTER PHILATELIC SOCIETY." The central design is of a statue of an old-time mariner at the wheel of a sailing vessel. Four different proof sheets were done on white paper using red, green, blue and purple inks–one color per sheet (REF#5660/20).

1934–New Jersey Philatelic Federation
12   perf and imperf   P3100 (photo)

The New Jersey Philatelic Federation of Newark, N.J., issued these items for its STAMPEX. The border inscription reads, "NEW JERSEY STATE STAMP SHOW 4TH ANNUAL STAMP EXHIBITION N.J. PHILATELIC FEDERATION-NEWARK-1934." The central design of George Washington crossing the Delaware River is printed in black in a circular area surrounded by a design of oak leaves and two busts. The design is printed on white paper in eight different colors with there being four colors on each sheet of stamps. Each individual stamp is printed in one color, with all having the black printed centers. One sheet is printed with red, blue, green, and purple stamps such that a block of four stamps, with their apexes meeting in the center, contains one of each color. The second sheet is printed using orange, pale blue, pale green, and a prussian blue. The two different colored sheets are in perforated form.

How many imperf items were issued is unclear. I suspect the imperf form also exists for both color schemes, but have as yet not been able to prove it. I am still looking for confirmation via finding an orange imperf item (REF#5660/28).

P3100

P3080   P3120

1934–Suburban Collectors Club
4   imperf   P3120 (photo)

This issue has a colored border area inscribed, "FEB 22-23-24-25 1934," in one of four colors with a central design also in one of four colors. The central design is outlined with a border reading, "SUBURBAN COLLECTORS CLUB-3RD ANNUAL EXHIBIT RIVERSIDE ILL. PUBLIC LIBRARY." The central design is of the Riverside Water Tower. The color combinations currently known are a green border with a purple design, orange border and black design, purple with red, and brown with blue.

1935–Hawthorne Stamp Club
3   imperf   P3140 (photo)

The Hawthorne Stamp Club of Cicero, Ill. produced imperf sheets of four identical stamps in three different colorings on white paper: purple and orange, green and orange, green and pale green (REF#5660/20).

P3140

P3160

Country	Year	Item			Mint	Used	Cover
	No. in set	Separation	Item Number				
Description							

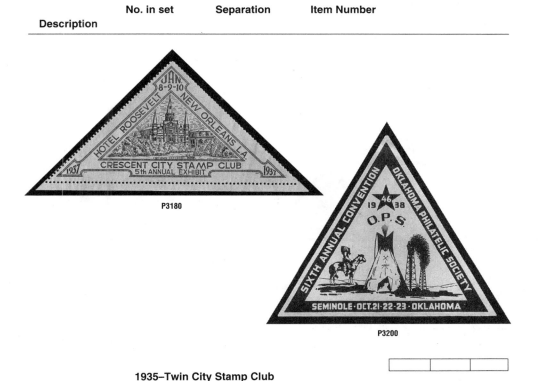

P3180

P3200

1935–Twin City Stamp Club
3   imperf   P3160 (photo)

This issue on white paper has a border inscription, "TWIN CITY STAMP CLUB Monroe, Louisiana." The central design is three lines of lettering, "FIRST EXHIBITION May 23–1935." One of the items is printed in green. I have no information on the colors of the other two items (REF#5660/48).

1937–Crescent City Stamp Club
8   perf and imperf   P3180 (photo)

The Crescent City Stamp Club of New Orleans, La. issued both a perf and imperf set of four items each with green and brown printing on white paper. These are large items with each stamp being 4-3/8 inches wide by 2-3/16 inches high. The borders are inscribed, "HOTEL ROOSEVELT NEW ORLEANS LA. CRESCENT CITY STAMP CLUB 5TH ANNUAL EXHIBIT JAN 8-9-10 1937." There are four vignettes: The Chalmette Monument, the statue of Andrew Jackson, the St. Louis Cathedral, and the Dueling Oaks City Park. These were produced in sheets of four, with each sheet containing all four designs (REF#5660/16).

1938–Oklahoma Phil Society
1   imperf   P3200 (photo)

The Oklahoma Philatelic Society, Tulsa, Okla., issued a very large imperforate item for its sixth convention–the item is an equilateral triangle of 3-3/4 inches on each side. The borders contain the inscription, "SIXTH ANNUAL CONVENTION OKLAHOMA PHILATELIC SOCIETY SEMINOLE OCT 21-22-23 OKLAHOMA." The design is an Indian on horseback, a teepee, and oil wells spouting a gusher. It has black printing on bright orange paper (REF#5660/32).

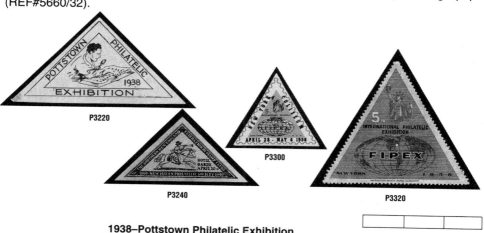

1938–Pottstown Philatelic Exhibition
4   imperf   **P3220 (photo)**

The Pottstown Stamp Club in Pottstown, Pa., issued these four imperf items. The border inscription reads, "POTTSTOWN PHILATELIC EXHIBITION." The central design is a stamp collector using a magnifying glass to look at stamps in an album. It was printed on white paper in four colors: black, blue, dark green, and brown. It came in sheets of four items, but whether a sheet contained only one or all four colors is not known (REF#5660/35)

1940–New Haven Philatelic Society
3   imperf   **P3240 (photo)**

These items were produced in imperforate sheets of four identical stamps. The border inscription reads, "THE SOUTHERN NEW ENGLAND FEDERATION OF STAMP CLUBS 1840 NEW HAVEN PHILATELIC SOCIETY 1940." The central vignette is of a galloping horse and rider, with the rider blowing a long trumpet-like horn. Three different colors of printing–blue, red (or is it orange?), and green–were used on white paper, with there being one color per sheet. There were two styles of sheets printed: one had the stamps with no other inscriptions, while the larger sheet had inscriptions outside the stamps (REF#5660/28).

1949–NY National ASDA Show
1   perf   **P3260**

A fairly common item is this label issued for the 1949 ASDA show in New York. The border reads, "NATIONAL POSTAGE STAMP SHOW NY NOV 18-19 & 20 1949 NY," with the central design being a stylized logo of ASDA. These equilateral items are deep purple printing on pink paper.

1950–Evansville Exhibition and Congress
3   imperf   **P3280**

These rather large items, 3 inch by 3-1/4 inch, are on colored paper, with borders outlined in the same color and printing in black ink. The design is lines of printed text which includes, "1950 EXHIBITION & CONGRESS EVANSVILLE, INDIANA HOTEL VENDOME

SEPT 29-30-OCT 1 TRI-STATE FEDERATION NFSC," and the three state names, "INDI-ANA KENTUCKY ILLINOIS." They exist in at least pink, blue, and green. (Are there other colors? Were these for a philatelic event or for some other kind of exhibition?)

1956–FIPEX-small size
1   imperf   P3300 (photo)

The fifth International Philatelic Exhibition held in New York in April-May 1956 issued two different commemorative labels. These smaller ones are imperf on white paper with a border inscription printed in black of, "NEW YORK COLISEUM APRIL 28-MAY 6 1956." The central vignette is in pale blue, with black printing depicting the Statue of Liberty and a global map of the world.

1956–FIPEX-large size
4   perf   P3320 (photo)

These larger items were perforated and printed on white paper in four pale colors–red, blue, green, and purple–one color per stamp. Although this stamp has no border, the design is the same as the central vignette used on the smaller label issued for this exhibition. (How were these items issued? Separate colors per full sheet or the four colors in blocks of four? How many stamps per full sheet?)

1956–MOKAEX
1   imperf   P3340 (photo)

The border of this imperf item is inscribed, "4 State Federation of Stamp Clubs MO-KAEX 1956 Little Rock, Arkansas Twin City Stamp Club, Host." The central design reads, "In Skyway HOTEL LAFAYETTE Sept. 21-22-23." Green paper was used with black printing. (Were other colors issued?)

P3340   P3360   P4060

1958–BAPEX
1   imperf   P3360 (photo)

The 1958 Bakersfield (California) Philatelic Exhibition issued an imperf item depicting a cornucopia with bales of hay, growing green leafy crops, oil wells, and mountain peaks in the background. The light blue printing on sand colored paper includes the inscription,"19 ~BAPEX ~ 58 AUGUST 30, 31-SEPTEMBER 1 ~ BAKERSFIELD INN, BAKERSFIELD, CALIFORNIA."

Country	Year	Item		Mint	Used	Cover
	No. in set	Separation	Item Number			
Description						

1992–Lundy Collector's Club
1 imperf P3380

The Lundy 1961 Europa souvenir sheet was reissued by the Lundy Collector's Club in 1992 at the World Colombian Stamp Expo'92. Additional printing was added at each end of the sheet to identify the "who" and "when" of the reissue.

Philatelica–organizations

DENMARK ?–Philatelic club
1 ? P4020

The Cape triangle is illustrated as the central vignette of this item printed in black on white paper. There is a wide pale aqua border inscribed in black, "FILATELISTKLUBBEN DANMARK HORSENS ABONNER PAA FRIMAERKETIDENDE."

SWEDEN late 1960s–Cinderella Club issue
1 perf P4040

The Swedish Cinderella Club has a triangular label as the club's own stamp. The stamp is a "reproduction" of the undenominated 1888 Goteborg local except its inscription is, "SAMLAR FÖRENINGEN BÄLTESPÄNNARNA." The vignette appears to be two or three intertwined standing figures, like a classical sculpture. The color(s) used are unknown to me.

USA 1935–Albuquerque Philatelic Society
1 imperf P4060 (photo)

This label has a stylized map of New Mexico as the central design on green paper with black printing and is inscribed, "ALBUQUERQUE PHILATELIC SOCIETY 1935."

Misc.–artistamps

Artistamps are generally in the nature of a personal commemorative label or seal issued by an individual, rather than an organization. Their topics are some personal events or statements the creator wishes to express. Usually the creator has not expected these "stamps" would be placed upon a letter or parcel. Many of the artistamps are beautiful, interesting, unique items. They are also very collectible.

For a comprehensive review of one artist's work, see REF#1326. This is an excellent representation of artistamps and their creator, and a fascinating book to read.

A significant cataloging of artist stamps is REF#5610. This work provides illustrations, issue information, and background when known on a large number of stamp artists works.

A classification difficulty arises between "modern local posts" and "artistamps." When does an item fit in one classification versus the other? "Local Posts" implies an association with some form of delivery service. In *Triangular Philatelics*, items produced by individuals labeled to indicate a "postal" service or where there is other evidence of the postal tie-in are classified as "local posts"–all others are classified as "artistamps."

M1	M1	M1	M1

Are these "real" philatelic items, or only art pieces? Each collector decides for themselves. The artistamps have not been created to authorize a delivery service. Personally, I do not consider them to be philatelic items, and thus do not include them in my own philatelic collection.

The existence of triangular-shaped artistamps makes the identification of Cinderella items more difficult. This section on artistamps is included to help with the identification of items you find. This is based primarily on recognizing key parts of the item's inscription. This will help you distinguish triangular artistamps from triangular Cinderallas.

Identifying inscription	Artist	Years	# Issues	# Items
Banana Post	Anna B.	1987, 1991	2	34
Betty's Fantasy	Beth Jacobsen	1994	1	1
Bug Post	Dominique Bugpost	1	8	
Canadada	Ed Varney	1990		
Doo Da Post; Edward F. Higgins	E.F. Higgins	1978-1993	9	7
GAIA NETWALK CONGRESS	Gerard Barbot	1991	1	2
Interplanetary Postal Essays	Modern Publications	1962	1	6
International Art Post '90	Banana Productions	1990	1	30
Kiss my art post Mars Sept 18 1993 Seattle	Beth Jacobson	1993	1	2
Kite Post	Francis Hall	1988-1992	several	several
Mars Expo '93	Joseph Klaffki	1993	1	12
Mondo Post 1	Ed Varney	1995	1	2
Mraur	Jas W. Felter	1990	1	2
Pacific Northwest Artistamp Collective	Anna B.	1990	1	4
Pan-American Visitation; Pan-American MailArt; Ambassador Zeppelin; Amazonia Earth Day 1990	Chuck Welch	1984, 1990	2	13
Republic of Mevu	GeirSor Reime	1995	1	2
Pre-Natal; Post-Natal; SOMA; Dogfish	Robert Rudine	1970-1996	11	11
Toast Postes	Greg Byrd	1992-1997		
TUZO 60c	Alison Baldwin	1993	1	16

Misc.–postal savings stamps

SPAIN **1916-1933–Post Office Savings Bank**
57 perf M2020 (photo)

From 1916 to 1933, the Spanish Post Office issued stamps and held the funds paid as a governmental savings program. These stamps were issued in sets (sheetlets?) of three perforated triangular stamps–one large stamp with two smaller ones on each side such that the three parts made up a rectangular shape. Each of the three parts was stamped with a single identifying serial number. (What use was made of the three parts? Are these considered Spanish revenues? What resource or article references them?)

M2020 M2020 M2020

There were four designs used over the total period:
- The first design was used from 1916 to 1925. It is distinguished by the central crown being distinct from the central area containing "ESPANA." The other three designs have a branch with leaves reaching up from the banner with "ESPANA" toward the crown.
- In the second design, the crown is a regal-shaped crown, with the traditional jeweled rounded central portion with a knob on top.
- In the third design, there is no crown.
- In the fourth design, the crown has a flat top, is angular, and has the appearance of four castle turrets.

The second through fourth designs were in use from 1926 to 1933 (REF#1726/243).

Galvez No.	Design group	Denomination	Colors
1	First	5c	black
2	First	25c	black bronze
3	First	1p	carmine
4	First	2p	violet
5	First	5p	yellow-ochre
6	First	10p	lilac
7	First	20p	orange
8	First	100p	green
9	First	500p	chestnut red
10	Second	1p	light red
11	Second	2p	gray violet
12	Second	5p	yellow
13	Second	50p	gray green
14	Second	500p	chestnut red
15	Third	5p	yellow
16	Fourth	10p	light violet
17	Fourth	25p	rose carmine
18	Fourth	100p	yellow green
19	Fourth	500p	chestnut violet

Country	Year	Item			Mint	Used	Cover
	No. in set	Separation	Item Number				
Description							

Misc.–postal stationery

Various businesses have created postal stationery, envelopes or postcards, with the postage pre-printed on the stationery. Some of these have been of a triangular item. Since these have not been issued by a governmental postal authority, they are Cinderella items, even though they are valid for use in the official postal system.

AUSTRALIA 1956–Melbourne
1 - M3020

This item depicts Saint George slaying a dragon. It is a 3d denomination by an unknown Melbourne firm (REF#8620 June 1978/92).

SOUTH AFRICA ?–Hout Bay
1 - M3040

Printed in bright mauve is a rough resemblance to the Cape triangle with the border inscribed, "POSTAGE PAID CAPE TOWN." The air mail envelope was issued by Harold Hollander, Philatelic Auctions, Hout Bay, South Africa.

Misc.–se-tenant tabs

Se-tenant tabs are labels printed along with postage stamps. Triangular tabs typically have no identification, nor any inscription to indicate who issued them and with what postal items. They are created for one of two reasons: either to make the full sheet value of the stamps a nice "even" amount, or to provide additional incentive for collectors to buy the stamps or sheets of stamps.

M4020   M4040   M4060

They are really curious items. Souvenir sheets and mini-sheets are the usual ways a postal service creates additional items for collectors. Also, the space used by a printed tab can more easily be left blank when getting the value of a full sheet to a desired amount.

ALBANIA 1973–Regular Mail - Flowering cactus issue
1 perf M4020 (photo)

There were eight items printed se-tenant and a block of eight stamps can have all different designs and denominations. However, a block of eight stamps may also have a tab instead of the 30q denomination stamp. The tab is printed in gold, with a design of finely spaced concentric arcs giving the appearance of plant leaves–very relevant since all eight stamps depict flowering cacti. The tab probably occurs once for every four sets of eight items, and undoubtedly was done to adjust the full sheet value.

Country	Year	Item		Mint	Used	Cover
	No. in set	Separation	Item Number			
Description						

COOK ISLANDS   1969–Regular Mail-South Pacific Games issue
          2   perf   M4040 (photo)

The Cook Islands issued a sheet of 10 stamps and two tabs for the Third South Pacific Games held in Port Morseby. Each of the 12 items has a colorful floral border on two of the sides, the base and one other side. The border on the stamps includes, "COOK ISLANDS," but the tabs do not have that inscription. The stamps were designed with the apex upward, whereas the tabs have the apex downward. One tab has a vignette of the coat of arms of New Zealand, and the other has a circular design inscribed, "PORT MORESBY III SOUTH PACIFIC GAMES."

MALI   1980–Air Post-Jules Verne issue
          4   perf   M4060 (photo)

Mali's set of four airmail stamps depict Jules Vern travel fantasy designs. They are composed of a stamp plus a tete beche, se-tenant label. The label is a drawing related to the theme of the stamps, but without any text or numbers. It is strictly added decoration. The tabs are printed in the same colors as the accompanying stamp. The tab depicts a modern event when the stamp depicts a Vern fantasy, and vice versa. The tabs have the appearance of stamp vignettes without any borders or inscriptions. Since there is a tab for every stamp, these were not produced to adjust the sheet value.

MARSHALL ISLANDS1997-Regular Mail-Hong Kong issue
          10   perf   M4080 (photo)

There are two sheets, each having two stamps and five triangular tabs. These sheets were issued to commemorate Hong Kong's change to the Chinese government. On each sheet, three of the tabs show part of the Hong Kong skyline scene. The other two relate to the sheet's production.

M4080

MONACO   1980–Postage Due-Knight in armor issue
          2   perf   M4100 (photo)

This Monaco set of 12 postage dues all have the same design. Each stamp's vignette is printed in a single different color. Between each two stamps was a triangular tab. The tab design is the Arms of Monaco–a large medieval crown with a knight standing on each side of it. The colors of the accompanying tabs are as follows:
- For the 0.05 through 1.00 denominations, the tab is carmine red, the same color as the border line on the 0.10 to 0.50 values.
- For the 2.00 to 5.00 denominations, the tab color is the same color as the vignette.

Country	Year	Item		Mint	Used	Cover
	No. in set	Separation	Item Number			
Description						

M4100   M4120   M4120

ROMANIA   1957–Regular Mail-Youth festival issue
         20   perf   M4120 (photo)

Romania issued a set of stamps to commemorate the 1957 Moscow Youth Festival. The triangular stamp was printed in sheets that included 20 different tabs. The triangular tabs say "Peace and Friendship" in 20 different languages.

RUSSIA   1966–Regular Mail-Winter Spartacist Games issue
         3   perf   M4140

Each of the three stamps in this Russian set has a tab attached. The tab is the upper triangle and the stamp is the lower triangle, with the pair forming a square. The two triangles are separated by perforations. The stamps all have the same design, only the colors and denomination differ. The tabs are three completely different designs printed using the same colors as on the accompanying stamp. The tabs depict three winter sport events: speed ice skating, ice hockey, and downhill skiing.

SPAIN   1930–Regular Mail-Christopher Columbus issue
         6   perf   M4160 (photo)

The three postage stamps were each printed in sheets of 25. The sheet included five tabs and a corner block stating the number of stamps and their denomination. The tabs are of two different designs–three with seven three-pointed cones radiating out from a central point, and two with a six-spoke central "wheel." The sheets are printed in only one color, the color of the stamp. Thus, there is a total of six different tabs (REF#1726/71).

M4160   M4160   M4180

         1992–Semipostal-Christopher Columbus issue
         1   perf souvenir sheet M4180 (photo)

This sheet has reproductions of the "classic" three Columbus triangles from the 1930 issue–only the denominations in the two lower corners have changed. The sheet also has a triangular tab printed in reddish brown depicting a statue of Columbus on top of a column.

UNITED STATES   1997–Regular Mail-Pacific 97 triangular issue
         4   perf   M4200 (photo)

The two transportation triangulars issued by the United States for Pacific 97, the international stamp show held in San Fransisco in 1997, were printed in sheets of six panes (with 16 stamps in a pane) separated by a horizontal gutter. The gutter contained 24 perforated triangular tabs in four different designs.

M4200

Misc.–toy stamps

PALOMBIA   **196?–from French children's paper**
         2   perf   M5020 (photo)

The French children's paper, *Journal De Spirou,* gave these items away with the paper sometime before 1970. The design is of a cartoon animal in dark blue on a background that appears like a maze. The inscription is, "JOURNAL DE SPIROU REPUBLICA de PALOMBIA." The blue stamp has a denomination of 1 and the red stamp has a 2. These could also be classified as "bogus" issues (REF#7660/40).

Misc.–triangular stamps-on-stamps

"Stamps-on-stamps" is a topical category. It refers to stamps that illustrate other stamps. "Triangular stamps-on-stamps" are those that illustrate triangular-shaped stamps. This section documents Cinderellas that depict triangular items. These stamps are themselves not triangular shaped.

GREAT BRITAIN   **1950–London International**
            1   imperf souvenir sheetM6020

Issued in conjunction with The London International Stamp Exhibition of 1950, this multi-color rectangular sheet, while not a triangle, does depict a classic 1853 Cape of Good Hope stamp, and four other non-triangular classics. The "depiction" is the same size as the real stamp, but fortunately the printing is of poorer quality and the paper is thinner. A nice stamp-on-stamp Cinderella (see the stamp-on-stamp section in this handbook).

            1956–Stanley Gibbons
            1   perf   M6040

This rectangular stamp, printed in purple on white paper, depicts a Cape of Good Hope triangular stamp. It is inscribed, "STANLEY GIBBONS LTD. EVERYTHING FOR PHILATELISTS." This stamp is one of two printed se-tenant. The other is an advertisement for the printing firm of Harrison & Sons Ltd., which printed the stamps.

            1960–London International
            1   imperf souvenir sheetM6060

Issued in conjunction with The London International Stamp Exhibition of 1960. This multi-color rectangular sheet, while not a triangle, does depict a classic 1861 Cape of Good

Hope stamp, and five other non-triangular classics. The "depiction" is slightly smaller than the real stamp. Another stamp-on-stamp Cinderella.

1971–Strike Post
1   roulette   M6080

Four U.K. special-delivery stamps to different parts of the world were printed in a mini-sheet. The one for delivery to Africa is illustrated with the 1953 4d South Africa postage stamp that depicts a Cape of Good Hope triangular.

USA   **1940–Brooklyn Stamp Club International**
1   imperf souvenir sheet M6100

A rectangular souvenir sheet printed in black on white paper has a replica of the Cape of Good Hope stamp with the border inscribed, "STAMP CLUB INTERNATIONAL." This sheet was issued for the club's 20th Anniversary. The sheet also has a Great Britain one penny black on it. (Did the club ever issue the imitation Cape as a separate stamp?)

Misc.–not classified

CZECHOSLOVAKIA ?–?
1   imperf   M7020 (photo)

This item has red borders and a red stripe across the center of a blue background. "SVAZ ZELEZNIKU STATU CESKOSLOVENSKEHO V PRAZE" is on five horizontal lines.

M7020   M7080   M7120

DENMARK   **?–Danmark Danebrog Danevirke**
1   imperf   M7040

This item's border area has blue lettering inscribed, "DANMARK DANEBROG DANEV-IRKE" around two mythic lions in blue on a red and brown background

GERMANY   **?–Lufthansa airline label**
1   imperf   M7060

This label is letter size rather than baggage size. It is printed in black on white paper and depicts the silhouette of a one-engine airplane as seen from above. The inscription is, "DEUTSCHE LUFTHANSA AG."

HUNGARY   **?–IBUSZ**
1   perf   M7080 (photo)

A yellow border with red printing surrounds a central emerald green background with two white sailboats. The central area is inscribed in black "IBUSZ." The border inscription is, "BESUCHEN SIE UNGARN BESUCHEN SIE UNGARN BALATON BALATON."

?–TANULOK
1   perf   M7100

In brown and green printing on white paper is a vignette of a duck flying from a pond with other ducks and reeds. The lower border is inscribed, "TANULÖK BALESETBIZTOSÏTÄSA."

1914-1916–dragonslayer
1   imperf   M7120 (photo)

The vignette in gray, red, and black is of a knight in armor on horseback over a slain dragon. It is inscribed, "1914-1916 MAGYAR, KUZDJ ES BIZVA BIZZAL!!"

1979–Allami Biztosito
1   perf   M7140

A multi-colored cartoon character of a young man dressed as an old -time knight with helmet, battle ax and shield is on a mustard-colored background. The inscription in black is, "30 ÉVES AZ ÁLLAMI BIZTOSÍTÓ 1979."

ICELAND   **1958–FRIMEX, Reykjavik**
1   perf   M7160

On an aqua background is a white outline map of Iceland and the image of a standing warrior(?) with an inscription in black, "FRIMEX REYKJAVIK 1958."

ITALY?   **?–Fiera Del Levante Bari**
1   perf   M7180

The vignette is the outline of an old-time sailing ship, printed in red, above a few blue wavy lines over the inscription, "FIERA DEL LEVANTE BARI 6-21 IX." All of that is oriented at 90 degrees to the longest side of the triangle. There is also the inscription "Visitateci nella Sezione Arredamento" printed along the longest side, so this stamp does not have a defined design orientation.

RUSSIA   **?–miniature of 1922 Semi-postal stamp**
1   imperf   M7200

This is a smaller version of the triangular Russian Semipostal of 1922. Like the full-size stamp, it is printed in red on white paper. The drawing is an outline of two hands clasped, two stalks of wheat, and a star. The sides are half the length of the actual semipostal stamp. (Does anyone know why they were produced?)

UNKNOWN   **1964–Newcastle Gliding Club**
1   imperf   M7220

The design, printed in blue on white paper, depicts a glider in flight with the outline of a cloud behind it. The bottom border inscription is, "Germania Posta 1964." In smaller lettering on the other borders is, "NEWCASTLE GLIDING CLUB."

Country	Year	Item			Mint	Used	Cover
	No. in set	Separation	Item Number				
Description							

?–Scandinavian?

1   imperf   **M7240**

On a yellow background with a red outline border is a central black inscription, "RAKNA MED GUD."

?–?

1   imperf   **M7260**

On a blue background with the white image of a hot spring's geyser shooting upward is inscribed, "Baderland Schlesien."

Chapter 12

Triangular Cinderella Finder

The table on the next several pages is an aid for your use in identifying Cinderella triangular stamps. When you want to identify a triangular item, first determine if it is a postage stamp or not. In cases where the identification is not established, use the table below to see if the stamp is a Cinderella cataloged in this handbook.

The Finder is an index to the Cinderella Listing. The keywords are in alphabetical order. Try to match part of the stamp's inscription with the keyword entries. When a match is found, the table provides the section and country where the stamp is catalogued. That entry will provide more information to use in making a positive identification of your stamp or label.

The table of contents below indicates the starting page of a each classification's detailed listings. The caption prefix is followed by three digits to give the identification number for an item. Those identification numbers are used as captions under the illustrations.

Keyphrase	Classification	Country
	Labels and seals–charity fund-raising	Russia
	Labels and seals–letter seals	Germany
	Labels and seals–publicity-prop.	Ukraine
	Labels and seals–ww-delandre	France
"VICTORY" repeated three times	Labels and seals–ww-patriotic	USA
100	Labels and seals–charity fund-raising	Unknown
19 ~BAPEX ~ 58	Philatelica–exhibitions	USA
1920 FAIRS	Labels and seals–publicity-commem.	Canada
1971 STRIKE POST	Locals–postal strike	Great Britain
3 TUG	Labels and seals–publicity-advert.	USA
5.2.1905 Kornerbund	Labels and seals–publicity-commem.	Germany
60JAHRE V7B. BARMEN	Labels and seals–publicity-advert.	Germany
AEROVIAS PUERTO RICO	Other airmail–essay and semi-off.	Puerto Rico
ALBUQUERQUE PHILATELIC SOCIETY	Philatelica–organizations	USA
ÁLLAMI BIZTOSÍÓ" 1979	Misc.–not classified	Hungary
ALLEN REPRODUCTION COMPANY	Labels and seals–publicity-advert.	USA
ALPINER KLUB	Locals–pre-1950	Austria
AMERBEROLINA CO.	Philatelica–advertising	USA
ARCTIC Air Mercy Flight	Phantoms and bogus	USA
ATLANTIS	Phantoms and bogus	USA
AUSSTELLUNG DDR MARKKLEEBERG	Labels and seals–publicity-commem.	Germany
AUSTRALIA ROCKET FIRING	Other airmail–rocket mail	Australia
AUSTRALIA YOUNG ROCKET EXPERIM	Other airmail–rocket mail	Australia
BADERLAND SCHLESIEN	Misc.–not classified	Unknown
BANISH POVERTY	Labels and seals–ww-patriotic	USA
BEDFORD INDUSTRIES	Labels and seals–charity fund-raising	Australia
BENSON & HEDGES	Labels and seals–publicity-advert.	Australia
BERGEDORF	Locals–pre-1950	Germany
BERLIN	Locals–pre-1950	Germany
BEXHILL DELIVERY	Locals–postal strike	Great Britain
BOMBAY PHILATELIC CO	Philatelica–advertising	USA
BORGÅ-KERVO BANAN	Locals–railway	Finland
BORT MED RUSDRIKKENE	Labels and seals–publicity-prop.	Norway
BOSTON GIFT SHOW	Labels and seals–publicity-advert.	USA
BRUGG 1927	Other airmail–essay and semi-off.	Switzerland
BUY THE EMPIRE'S FRUIT	Labels and seals–publicity-advert.	South Africa
CAJA POSTAL DE AHORROS	Misc.–postal savings stamps	Spain
CAP BUDAPEST or CAP WIEN	Labels and seals–publicity-commem.	Austria/Hungary
CENTERPORT L.I.	Locals–modern	USA
CHESUHNCOOK LAKE	Locals–modern	USA
CHUB CAY CARRIER SERVICE	Locals–modern	Bahamas
CIRCULAR VERKEHR KOLN	Locals–pre-1950	Germany
CITY OF LONDON DELIVERY	Locals–postal strike	Great Britain
CLEVELAND ZOO	Locals–modern	USA
COLN A/RH 5-7 AUGUST 1911	Labels and seals–publicity-commem.	Germany
COLORADO GHOST POST	Locals–modern	USA
COLORADO LOCAL POST	Locals–modern	USA
CONTRIBUICAO INDUSTRIAL	Revenues	Azores
CONTRIBUICAO INDUSTRIAL	Revenues	Portugal
CRESCENT CITY STAMP CLUB	Philatelica–exhibitions	USA
CRUZ ROJA ARGENTINA	Labels and seals–charity fund-raising	Argentina
CZY ZASZCZEPILES	Labels and seals–charity fund-raising	Poland
D.A.BERRY	Philatelica–advertising	Great Britain

Keyphrase	Classification	Country
DANMARK DANEBROG DANEVIRKE	Misc.–not classified	Denmark
DAVIS LOCAL POST	Locals–modern	USA
DE BOUZEK ENGRAVING	Labels and seals–publicity-advert.	USA
DEUTSCHE LUFTHANSA AG	Misc.–not classified	Germany
Deutschen in Galizipu	Labels and seals–publicity-commem.	Ukraine
DISPENSAIRE ANTITUBERCULEUX	Labels and seals–charity fund-raising	Switzerland
Dr.A.J.deBRUIJN RAKET POST	Other airmail–rocket mail	Luxembourg
DUNANTULI MEHESZETI KIALLITAS	Labels and seals–publicity-commem.	Hungary
DUTCH FIELD POST LETTER SEAL	Labels and seals–ww-other military	Holland/G.B.
ED.S.ESTOPPEY	Philatelica–advertising	Switzerland
EDUARD DRESSLER	Labels and seals–publicity-advert.	Germany
EMERGENCY MAIL	Locals–postal strike	Great Britain
ENGINEERS ARE PEOPLE	Labels and seals–publicity-advert.	USA
ENOTRIA LOCAL POST	Locals–modern	USA
ERSTE RAKCTEN FLUG	Other airmail–rocket mail	Liechtenstein
ESPERIMENTI DI POSTA	Other airmail–rocket mail	Italy
ESPERIMENTO POSTERASZZO	Other airmail–rocket mail	Italy
ESTES PARK LOCAL POST	Locals–modern	USA
ETATES DE JERSEY	Revenues	Jersey
EUCHARISTIC CONGRESS 1964	Labels and seals–publicity-commem.	India
EUROPA UNITA FORTIS EST	Labels and seals–publicity-advert.	Switzerland
EXPOSITION 1897 BRUXELLES	Labels and seals–publicity-advert.	Belgium
FABIAN'S PHANTOM POST	Locals–modern	USA
FIERA DEL LEVANTE BARI	Misc.–not classified	Italy
FIGHT CANCER PENNY HEALTH	Labels and seals–charity fund-raising	USA
FILATELISTKLUBBEN DANMARK	Philatelica–organizations	Denmark
FOIRE MESSE FAIR	Labels and seals–publicity-commem.	Hungary
FOR TICKET INFORMATION	Labels and seals–publicity-advert.	USA
FORT FINDLAY	Locals–modern	USA
FOURTH PHILATELIC CONGRESS	Philatelica–exhibitions	Great Britain
FRANCE AMERIQUE FONDATION BYRD	Labels and seals–publicity-advert.	France
FRANCIS J. FIELD	Philatelica–advertising	Great Britain
FRANCISCAN MISSIONARY	Labels and seals–charity fund-raising	USA
FRANKFURT	Locals–pre-1950	Germany
FRANKFURTER BUCHMESSE	Labels and seals–publicity-commem.	Germany
FRANZ JOSEPH LAND	Phantoms and bogus	Austria
FREE IRELAND	Labels and seals–publicity-prop.	Ireland
FRIMÄRKETS DAG	Philatelica–exhibitions	Sweden
FRIMEX REYKJAVIK	Misc.–not classified	Iceland
GERMANA ESPERANTA KONGRESO	Labels and seals–publicity-commem.	Germany
GERMANIA Posta 1964	Misc.–not classified	Unknown
GIBBONS STAMP WEEKLY	Philatelica–advertising	Great Britain
GLOUCESTER PHILATELIC SOCIETY	Philatelica–exhibitions	USA
GOD BLESS AMERICA OR HAPPY LANDING OR HOLIDAY WISHES OR NOEL	Labels and seals–letter seals	USA
GOOD SHEPHERD LOCAL POST	Locals–modern	USA
GORKAU	Revenues	Czechoslovakia
GRAHAM CAREY SPECIAL	Philatelica–commemorative	Australia
GRAND DUCHY OF BARRE	Locals–modern	USA
GREAT BARRIER PIGEON POST	Philatelica–commemorative	New Zealand
GREAT BARRIER ISLAND	Other airmail–pigeon post	New Zealand
GREETINGS	Labels and seals–charity fund-raising	USA

Keyphrase	Classification	Country
GUGH ISLAND	Locals–modern	Great Britain
H.A. KENNEDY& CO.	Philatelica–advertising	Great Britain
H.K.IInT	Revenues	Russia
HABILITACION, BIENIO	Revenues	Colombia
HAWTHORNE STAMP CLUB	Philatelica–exhibitions	USA
HERM ISLAND	Locals–modern	Great Britain
HEYST A/ZEE DUINBERGEN	Other airmail–rocket mail	Belgium
HINTON DERBY DAYS	Labels and seals–publicity-advert.	Canada
HISTORICAL PAGEANT OF SOUTH AFRICA	Labels and seals–publicity-advert.	South Africa
HOWARD LOCAL POST	Locals–modern	USA
HUERFANOS DEL CUERPO	Labels and seals–charity fund-raising	Spain
HUSKVARNA LOKALT	Locals–pre-1950	Sweden
IBUSZ	Misc.–not classified	Hungary
ILE ROY	Phantoms and bogus	France
INTERNATIONAL FAIR, BRUSSELS	Labels and seals–publicity-advert.	Belgium
INTERNATIONAL ROCKET FLIGHT	Other airmail–rocket mail	USA
ISLAND	Other airmail–rocket mail	Iceland
ITALIAN EARTHQUAKE	Labels and seals–charity fund raising	USA
JOKAI CENTENNARIUMA	Labels and seals–publicity-commem.	Hungary
JOURNAL DE SPIROU	Misc.–toy stamps	Palombia
JUGOSI EDELMESSE STUTTGART	Labels and seals–publicity-advert.	Germany
KARL-MARX-STAD	Labels and seals–publicity-commem.	Germany
KERNOW	Labels and seals–publicity-prop.	Great Britain
KERSTMIS-NEDERLAND	Labels and seals–charity fund-raising	Netherlands
KHOR FAKKAN	Phantoms and bogus	Khor Fakkan
KREFELDER VERKEHRS:	Labels and seals–publicity-commem.	Germany
KUZDJ ES BIZVA BIZZAL	Misc.–not classified	Hungary
LAND'S END	Labels and seals–publicity-advert.	Great Britain
LARK LOCAL POST	Locals–modern	USA
LE CENTENAIRE DA LA CONFEDERATION	Labels and seals–publicity-commem.	Canada
LEITMERITZ ED. HOFER	Locals–pre-1950	Czechoslovakia
LIBERALE 2PF	Labels and seals–publicity-prop.	Germany
LIGA ARGENTINA CONTRA LA TUBERCULOSIS	Labels and seals–charity fund-raising	Argentina
LOCAL POST GBI AAF-IRC	Locals–modern	Bahamas
LOKAL POST GOTEBORG	Locals–pre-1950	Sweden
LONDON INTERNATIONAL STAMP EXHIBITION OF 1950	Philatelica–exhibitions	Great Britain
LONDON INTERNATIONAL STAMP EXHIBITION OF 1960	Philatelica–exhibitions	Great Britain
LUNDY	Locals–modern	Great Britain
MAHENO-FRASER ISLAND	Other airmail–rocket mail	Australia
MCLP	Locals-modern	USA
MEMBER ROCHESTER YMCA	Labels and seals–charity fund-raising	USA
MOHÁCS 1926	Labels and seals–publicity-commem.	Hungary
MOKAEX 1956	Philatelica–exhibitions	USA
MONDA CAMPIONECO SVEDUJO	Labels and seals–publicity-commem.	Sweden
MONTHLY JOURNAL	Philatelica–advertising	Great Britain
MOTHERS DAY	Labels and seals–publicity-advert.	USA
MOUNTAINVILLE	Locals–Modern	USA
MRS. CHURCHILL'S FUND	Labels and seals–ww-patriotic	USA
N.D. HRVATSKA	Labels and seals–publicity-prop.	Croatia

Keyphrase	Classification	Country
NACHNAHME REMBOURSEMENT	Labels and seals–etiquettes-COD	Germany
NATIONAL PARKS AIRWAYS	Labels and seals–etiquettes-airmail	USA
NATIONAL POSTAGE STAMP SHOW	Philatelica–exhibitions	USA
NEDERLAND BELGIQUE DEUTSCHLAND	Other airmail–rocket mail	Belgium
NEDERLAND SE RAKETTENVLUCHT	Other airmail–rocket mail	Holland
NEDERLANDSCHE CENTRALE	Labels and seals–charity fund-raising	Netherlands
NEDERLANDSCHE POSTZEGEL	Labels and seals–publicity-commem.	Holland
NEDERLANDSCHE RAKETTENPOST	Other airmail–rocket mail	Holland
NEDERLANDSCHE VELDPOST	Labels and seals–ww-other military	Holland/G.B.
NEW HAVEN PHILATELIC SOCIETY	Philatelica–exhibitions	USA
NEW JERSEY STATE STAMP	Philatelica–exhibitions	USA
NEW YORK COLISEUM	Philatelica–exhibitions	USA
NOBLAIS	Labels and seals–charity fund-raising	Ireland
NRS	Other airmail–rocket mail	Holland
OBERAMMERGAU 1950	Labels and seals–publicity-advert.	Germany
OCONOMOWOC	Locals–modern	USA
OKLAHOMA PHILATELIC SOCIETY	Philatelica–exhibitions	USA
ORTHODOX JEWISH FAIR	Labels and seals–charity fund-raising	USA
OS ANIMALS SOFREM	Labels and seals–charity fund-raising	Portugal
PAR AVION	Labels and seals–etiquettes-airmail	France
PARIS 1900 PANORAMA	Labels and seals–publicity-advert.	France
PATRONATO DE LEPROSOS	Labels and seals–charity fund-raising	Argentina
PECIIYb^NKA TbIBA TUVA	Phantoms and bogus	Tanna Tuva
PÀCMAKSA REMBOURSEMENT	Labels and seals–etiquettes-COD	Latvia
PESHTIGO, WISCONSIN	Labels and seals–publicity-commem.	USA
PHILUMA PHILIPS	Labels and seals–publicity-advert.	Unknown
POOCH LOCAL POST	Locals–modern	USA
POR AVION	Labels and seals–etiquettes-airmail	Spain
POSTAGE PAID CAPE TOWN	Misc.–postal stationery	South Africa
POSTDAM 28 SEPT-2 OCT, 1901	Labels and seals–publicity-advert.	Germany
POSTFÖRSKOTT	Labels and seals–etiquettes-COD	Sweden
POSTSEGELFLUG ELCHINGEN	Labels and seals–publicity-commem.	Italy
POTTSTOWN PHILATELIC EXHIBITION	Philatelica–exhibitions	USA
PRIVAT-STADT POST, STUTTGART	Locals–pre-1950	Germany
PRO FOUNDATION ECONOMIA ETHIOPIA	Labels and seals–publicity-advert.	Ethiopia
PRO-NERJA	Revenues	Spain
PROVINZIAL OBST AUSSTELLUNG	Labels and seals–publicity-commem.	Germany
PUEBLA CIUDAD FERIA	Labels and seals–publicity-commem.	Unknown
QUAITI STATE IN HADHRAMAUT	Locals–modern	Quaiti
QUINQUE ET VIGINTI ANNI	Labels and seals–publicity-commem.	Unknown
RAKET POST	Other airmail–rocket mail	Holland
RAKETEN.VEREIN eV.AUGSBURG	Other airmail–rocket mail	Germany
RAKETENFLUGPOST IN OESTERREICH	Other airmail–rocket mail	Austria
RAKETENVLIEGTUIG PROEF IN NEDERLA	Other airmail–rocket mail	Holland
RAKETVLUCHT	Other airmail–rocket mail	Germany
RAKNA MED GUD	Misc.–not classified	Unknown
RATTLESNAKE ISLAND	Locals–modern	USA
REMBOURSEMENT	Labels and seals–etiquettes-COD	Sweden
REMBOURSEMENT	Locals–pre-1950	Germany
REPUBLICA DE CUBA CORREO AEREO	Other airmail–essay and semi-off.	Cuba
REPUBLICA DEL ECUADOR	Other airmail–essay and semi-off.	Ecuador
REPUBLIK MALUKU SELATAN	Labels and seals–publicity-prop.	RMS
RICHWOOD'S DISPATCH	Locals–pre-1950	USA

Keyphrase	Classification	Country
ROCKET POST IN ENGLAND	Other airmail–rocket mail	Great Britain
ROCKETFLIGHT LONDON	Other airmail–rocket mail	Great Britain
RRI ROCKETPOST	Other airmail–rocket mail	USA
S. AFRICAN INTERNATIONAL	Philatelica–exhibitions	South Africa
SALEM CHERRY FESTIVAL	Labels and seals–publicity-advert.	USA
SALZBURG 3-6 JULI 1930	Labels and seals–publicity-commem.	Austria
SAMLAR FÖRENINGEN BÄLTESPÄNNAR	Philatelica–organizations	Sweden
SANDIA CREST	Locals–modern	USA
SANGATTE·1935	Other airmail–rocket mail	France
SATELLITE BEACH	Locals–modern	USA
SAVE FOR VICTORY	Labels and seals–ww-patriotic	USA
SECRETARIA DE HACIENDAY TESORO	Revenues	Panama
See detail listing in text	Labels and seals–ww-Swiss Army	Switzerland
See listing	Misc.–artistamps	Various
SERVICE TOGETHER	Labels and seals–ww-other military	USA
SERVICO AEROPOSTAL REPUBLICA DEL PARAGUAY	Other airmail–essay and semi-off.	Paraguay
SHRUB OAK	Locals–modern	USA
SICILIA	Labels and seals–charity fund-raising	Italy
SOMERSET HOSPITAL	Labels and seals–charity fund-raising	South Africa
SOSNOWICE	Locals–pre-1950	Poland
SPOKAN FALLS LOCAL POST	Locals–modern	USA
STADTBRIEFBEF. zu HAMBURG	Locals–pre-1950	Germany
STAMP CLUB INTERNATIONAL	Philatelica–organizations	USA
SUBURBAN COLLECTORS CLUB	Philatelica–exhibitions	USA
SUISSE-EUROPE CENTRALE	Other airmail–essay and semi-off.	Switzerland
SUISSE-FRANCE	Other airmail–essay and semi-off.	Switzerland
SVAZ ZELEZNIKU STATU	Misc.–not classified	Czechoslovakia
TAFALLA BENE~FICENCIA	Revenues	Spain
TANULÖK BALESETBIZTOSÏTÄSA	Misc.–not classified	Hungary
TOKYO 1964	Labels and seals–publicity-commem.	Japan
TRI-STATE FEDERATION NFSC	Philatelica–exhibitions	USA
TWIN CITY STAMP CLUB	Philatelica–exhibitions	USA
USE SALVADOR COFFEE	Labels and seals–publicity-advert.	Salvador, El
UTASELLATO	Labels and seals–publicity-commem.	Hungary
Various airmail terms	Other airmail–essay and semi-off.	Unknown
Various slogans	Labels and seals–ww-patriotic	USA
VIA AÉREA	Labels and seals–etiquettes-airmail	Spain
VINCENNES	Other airmail–essay and semi-off.	France
W. RUSSELL	Philatelica–advertising	Holland
WAKEFIELD SUOMI FINLAND	Labels and seals–publicity-commem.	Finland
WATCH FOR OUR CHRISTMAS MESSAGE	Labels and seals–publicity-advert.	USA
WAUKESHA, WIS.	Locals–modern	USA
WEST SIDE YMCA	Labels and seals–charity fund-raising	USA
WHAT WALLA WALLA WANTS	Labels and seals–publicity-advert.	USA
WILL IT HELP TO WIN THE WAR	Labels and seals–ww-patriotic	USA
WORLD SKI CHAMPIONSHIP	Labels and seals–publicity-commem.	USA
YMCA 1941 WORLD	Labels and Seals–charity fund-raising	USA
ZAPISZ SIE NA	Labels and seals–charity fund-raising	Poland

Chapter 13

Philatelic Terminology

One of the nice pluses from collecting triangular stamps is their encompassing so many of the philatelic characteristics of stamps. This section of the handbook provides a glossary of philatelic terms pertinent to triangulars.

Added markings–At times the postal service has added printed or stamped information onto existing stamps. These markings were not on the originally printed stamps. They were applied by hand-stamping or running finished sheets through an additional printing process. These added markings change the price or intended use of the stamps.

> **Overprints**–Here the markings change some aspect of the stamp other than the denomination. Often done to reflect that a ruler has been deposed; to have the stamps commemorate some event; to indicate an occupation of the country in war; or to honor a change in government.

> **Surcharges**–This type of marking changes the face value of the stamp. The change may be due to a rapid increase in postal rates; a shortage of a particular value due to supply problems; a change in language and/or currency after losing a war. The revised denomination is usually printed on top of the old value. However, the old values may also be "blotted" out with the new amount being printed anywhere on the stamp.

> Due to the process used in reprinting, it is not unusual to get inverted overprints or surcharges. The overprints or surcharges may occur in different color inks from different press runs. Whether any of these printing variations affect the value depends on the scarcity of the variation. Collecting the variations adds to the completeness of your collection.

Bisect–Part of a higher-value stamp used for lower value postage. These were usually created by cutting a stamp into two or more parts. See the bisect section in Chapter 5 for a more complete discussion and illustrations.

Bourse–A bourse (or stamp show) is a get-together of dealers and collectors to buy, sell or trade stamps.

Cancellations–The markings postal authorities add to the stamp when it is used. This prevents the stamp from being used again without an appropriate payment to the postal service. Cancellations are usually a dark ink stamping, but can be anything that "defaces" the unused condition of the original stamp.

Catalog value–A price quoted in a standard stamp catalog. It is a good guide to use in determining the range you might expect to pay.

Centering–Refers to the placement of the stamp's printing on the physical paper. When the margins around the printed part of the stamp are all equal, the stamp is "centered." Nicely centered stamps are usually more valuable than ones with poor centering.

Cinderella–These are the stamps not included in the categories of postage stamps, souvenir sheets or revenue stamps. They have very wide, diverse reasons for having been made and used. The term "Cinderella" encompasses all these other kinds of items as a type of shorthand reference.

Classic–In general refers to a stamp more than 100 years old. Also it can refer to specific items that are well-known, rare and valuable.

Condition (of the stamp)

Mint or Unused–Refers to a stamp that remains as it was manufactured. It is in pristine condition with the original gum.

Used–A stamp that has gone through the postal-delivery process. A used stamp has a cancellation and the gum is either gone or the stamp is on another piece of paper , like an envelope.

CTO–Refers to mint stamps the postal service has canceled *without* the stamp having been used for postal purposes. These are mass canceled in full sheets by a printing operation of a pseudo-cancellation mark. Usually has been done to create stamps for sale to collectors, often by countries that produce many more stamps than their citizens can use. They have done this to make "used" stamps available for the collector, but as you can see they are not postally used stamps. Often they still have gum on the back of the stamp, which is quite a trick for a stamp that has been "used."

Covers–This is a complete envelope. It includes the postage stamp and a cancellation to indicate its processing for delivery by the postal authority in at least the country of origin. It may include additional cancellations to signify special circumstances regarding the delivery.

There are three main groupings of covers: Those arising from a legitimate postal use; those specially issued on the first day a stamp is available to the public (called First Day Covers); and those where the cover is created for other philatelic purposes (i.e. all the stamps in a set are used even though thay exceed the amount of postage required for the delivery service). The illustration page, Triangular Covers, shows an example of each of these groups.

Denomination–The price of the stamp as printed on the stamp.

Design–The printing on the stamp. A triangular's design usually has two parts–the vignette and the border.

Errors–A mistake made during the manufacture of the stamp. Part of the production did not happen as intended. Images could be upside down or shifted from where they were supposed to be printed. A wrong color could have been used, or one or more colors may have been omitted. Part of the design or the border may not have been printed. The perforations could be done in the wrong place or unintentionally be missing. All these are errors and if few enough of the stamps made it into circulation, then the error will often have a greatly raised value from its non-error counterpart.

Essay–A proposed design for a stamp, often in the form of a stamp.

Hinged–Refers to a stamp that at one time was mounted by a stamp hinge. This would usually be of concern for mint stamps, since the hinging process will damage the gum on the back of the stamp and thus lower the stamp's value.

Imperforate–See Separations.

Item–Either a stamp or label. This book uses this general term since many Cinderella items are not stamps, but are labels. So "item" refers to either.

Margin–The space between the outer edge of the printing and the physical edge of the stamp.

Mini-sheet–This is a sheet of stamps, smaller than the sheets produced for the main sales of the stamp(s), issued for collectors. A mini-sheet contains a small number of stamps, usually from one to 12. Usually each sheet has a few of *only* one item in the issue, with a separate mini-sheet for each item in the set. However, some mini-sheets contain one copy of each item in the issued set. Unlike souvenir sheets, mini-sheets do not have additional illustrations or commemorative inscriptions.

Multi-stamp layouts

These terms apply to two or more stamps still joined together as issued. The illustration page, Triangular Pairs, provides four examples of these terms.

Pair–Two stamps never separated.

Imperf pair–This is when the separator between the stamps is imperforate. When a stamp comes in both perf and imperf varieties, the imperf pair is the sure way to tell the stamp was originally issued as an imperf. With these issues, it is possible for someone to have trimmed away the perf holes of a perf stamp to create an imperf. This occurs when very few of the imperf were originally produced, making them hard to find or expensive. A way to tell is to check that the imperf is larger than the size of the perf stamp measured between the holes–both the full width and height need to be there.

Se-Tenant pair–Refers to stamps of different designs being produced next to each other. When a set of stamps contains multiple designs, the designs could have been produced one per sheet of stamps; or they could have been produced with more than one design occurring on the same sheet. The latter situation is a se-tenant sheet. The collector may desire to get an unseparated strip that contains one of each design in the issue to show the se-tenant condition. Unfortunately, this is harder for dealers to store and handle than individual stamps, so you will find it hard to get se-tenant strips.

Tete-beche pair–Refers to two adjacent stamps where the design in one is upside down relative to the other. Once separated, one cannot tell the stamps were printed tete-beche. Neither stamp has any printing that is upside down on the single stamp. Obviously, the collector needs to obtain an unseparated pair to portray this philatelic condition. This term comes from the French for "head the wrong way."

The "super" triangle–Refers to a group of unseparated stamps, where the shape of the set of stamps is itself a triangle. Whether this can occur for an item depends on the arrangement of the triangles on the original sheet being manufactured. It takes a minimum of four stamps to make a super-triangle; that is, one on the top, one in the center, one on the right side, and one on the left side.

Perforated–See Separations.

Philately–Refers to the serious collecting and study of stamps; and the study of postal services and their history.

Postal Stationery–Items produced and sold by the postal service such as envelopes, postal cards, air letters, etc., which were embossed or printed with the postal amount so the use of a stamp is normally not required.

Proof–A trial printing of a stamp's final design. This may be in different color inks or have a different separation than the final stamp.

Reprints–Stamps printed from the original plates after the stamps have been discontinued for postal use. This is done to make them available for collectors. Reprints can usually be identified through differences in paper or gum, or in color from the original issued stamps. They are invalid for postal use.

Roulette–See Separations.

Separations

Refers to the characteristic of a sheet of stamps for how they have been manufactured regarding the detachment of individual stamps.

Perforate–A stamp where tiny holes between the stamps help in separating one from another. In the manufacture of stamps, this was first used in the 1850s. It has become the overwhelmingly dominant way for achieving separation, since no special tool is required to get a quick separation of one stamp from another. Perforated stamps are referred to as "perfs." The spacing of the holes is measured in terms of the number of holes in a 2-centimeter length. There are numerous perf gauges available to help in measuring the perf size. Reference catalogs list the perf sizes for perforated stamps to aid in identification of the item.

Imperforate–A stamp that has no perforations. These are referred to as "imperfs." They were cut apart by the selling post office when individual stamps were bought, or by the letter sender when multiple stamps had been purchased.

Roulette–A separation method in which tiny slits are made between the stamps. No paper is removed in this process. It was invented in 1847, before perforators, but the machines' slitters wore out very quickly.

Additional note: The triangulars of Obock and the Somali Coast have a very interesting separation style. From 1893-1902, the stamps are imperforate with a printed perforation line around the outside of the stamp's border. These are unique and beautiful items.

Set–A complete group of stamps having a similar design or where the design follows a single consistent theme; for example, an issuance of Presidential portraits. A set does not have to be issued on a single date, although they most often are.

Souvenir Sheet–An item issued by postal services primarily for stamp collectors. They usually promote or commemorate some particular event. They often contain more than one stamp and usually have commemorative information printed around the stamps. They usually do not contain more than one copy of each stamp. Also see **Mini-sheet**.

Specimen–A stamp overprinted with a word meaning "specimen." These stamps were usually distributed to authorities and important personages as samples of a soon-to-be-issued stamp.

Tab–A label without postal validity which originally came with valid postage stamps. Also sometimes called a coupon. Tabs may be used to convey a message, or they may merely be decorated space fillers. The tabs themselves are a Cinderella item and listed in the category, Misc.–se-tenant tabs.

Tear–A break in a stamp that's usually a rip, but can be a cut. This greatly decreases a stamp's value.

Thin–Where part of a layer of the stamp's paper has been removed. This occurs on the back of hinged or used stamps due to their incorrect removal from wherever they were stuck.

Topicals–Topical collecting is when the collecting is of a particular subject. Some common subjects are mushrooms, space, aircraft, sports, Kennedy and Disney. Others will define their own topical collection to be a narrower subject, such as dirigibles rather than all aircraft, or rowing rather than all sports. Topical collecting is an alternative to collecting a particular country, either in whole or for a specific time period; to collecting only a particular kind of stamp; or to collecting worldwide issues. In Great Britain, this is called "thematics" collecting.

Vignette–The main picture on the stamp; the person depicted or the scene or whatever is on the stamp that makes up the main image. In older stamps, a border was often placed around the vignette to complete the design of the stamp.

Want List–A list of stamps you are trying to find; that is, the ones you "want." You will need a "master" want list of everything you are seeking. You will also prepare parts of that list for sending to dealers when ordering approvals by mail.

Chapter 14

Advanced Angles

This chapter contains miscellaneous information important to the collector who has, or wants to, advance from just collecting the stamps to the philatelics of the triangular item. "Philatelics" has two main components to its meaning–stamps and study. The sections below relate to the "study" aspect of the triangular item–the gaining and development of information and understanding related to the stamps.

Research materials

The information in this section is for those of you interested in doing more research on triangulars. *Triangular Philatelics* provides an excellent starting point since it includes a complete bibliography of the sources used in developing its contents.

Finding information about triangulars is not done by going to articles or books and finding a section devoted to the triangular topic. This handbook is probably the first which has specifically addressed triangular philatelics.

Articles or books on stamps in general, on specific countries or specific philatelic topics, were reviewed for their having any possible information on triangular items. The triangular shape's distinctiveness really helps when searching through large amounts of material, so long as the material is suitably illustrated.

Of course, the best source for research information is a library. Public libraries of cities and counties, educational institution libraries and specialized philatelic libraries are all worth visiting. With inter-library loans, you can get almost anything if you can locate which lending library has the material. A "non-lending library" does not circulate their materials–the material must be used in the library itself.

Some of the larger philatelic libraries in the USA are:

- American Philatelic Research Library, 100 Oakwood Avenue, State College, PA 16803.
- American Revenue Association Library, c/o George McNamara Jr., PO Box 136, Nora Springs, IA 50458
- Cardinal Spellman Philatelic Museum, 235 Wellesley Street, Weston, MA 02193.
- Idaho Stamp Collectors Library, 5612 W. State Street, Boise, ID 83703.
- The Collectors Club, 22 East 35th Street, New York, NY 10016.
- Western Philatelic Library, 1550 Partridge Avenue, Sunnyvale, CA 94086.
- Wineburg Philatelic Research Library, Box 643, University of Texas, Richardson, TX 75083.

This handbook's content is highly dependent on the research of printed material. This has an associated phenomenon that places limits on the completeness of the information. The phenomenon is that a printed source is only complete up to the date of its writing. This effect is negligible on the postage-stamp section, since most reference sources update frequently, even annually. However, the Cinderella references seldom are reissued in contemporary editions, probably because most of them have been written by individuals, rather than by an ongoing business. This means we have limited information on any new issues occurring during the period from the date of the reference up to the current time. For example, the major source of information on Rocket Mail is the Ellington-Zwisler Rocket Mail Catalog. This was written before 1973. Thus, any triangular rocket mail items issued after 1973 are probably missing from the listings in this handbook.

Original research

The advanced philatelist who collects Cinderellas is likely to come across unrecognized items. This presents the opportunity for doing research in the philatelic literature to develop information about the item. When that fails, one can attempt original research by reviewing old newspapers, writing to different historical societies, using old directories (telephone and city), contacting individuals or their descendants, or finding a way to get a translation of an inscription.

Chapter 15

Appendix

Reviewing statistics about triangulars helps in developing an understanding of the role they have played in the history of philately.

These statistics are for the triangular postage stamps issued from 1853-1996. These statistics exclude proofs, essays, errors, reprints and souvenir sheets.

An issue is defined as being created when there is some aspect to the set of stamps that differs from previous issues. This might be the color, design or denomination. Overprints and surcharges do create new issues since there was a postal need for the particular "added printing," done to eliminate designing and producing new stamps. When an item was issued with different separations (perforate, imperforate or roulette), it is counted as being only one issuance.

Triangular statistics by decade

Decade	No. of countries issuing	No. of issues	No. of stamps issued	No. of first issues
1850s	2	3	7	2
1860s	3	5	9	1
1890s	3	8	14	3
1900s	3	7	16	1
1910s	7	14	35	6
1920s	13	28	98	11
1930s	20	57	250	12
1940s	13	20	73	6
1950s	17	29	156	9
1960s	45	85	591	33
1970s	24	35	163	11
1980s	20	30	137	8
1990s	12	23	106	2
totals		344	1,655	105

The "number of issues" counts an issue done by a country when any stamp in the issue is a triangular. A "first issue" is when a country issues its first triangular stamp. For example, from 1900 to 1909, Ecuador issued five stamps in one set; Liberia issued five stamps in five sets and Somali Coast issued seven stamps in six sets. Thus, there were three countries that issued triangulars; 1908 was the first year for Ecuador having a triangular; there were 12 issues in the decade; and a total of 17 triangular stamps were created.

Statistics on the number of stamps does recognize the difference in separations. For example, when an item was produced in perforate and imperforate forms, this is counted as two stamps. For these statistics, both halves of a perforated bisect are included as one stamp.

Delivery service and frequency statistics

Type of mail service	No. of issues	No. of times issuing triangles	No. of countries
Regular mail	214	25	1
Air post	57	17	1
Official	15	14	1
Postage due	15	9	3
Semi-postal	15	8	5
Air post semi-postal	10	7	3
Personal delivery	4	6	1
Registered	3	5	4
Air post official	2	4	12
Newspaper	2	3	11
Parcel post	2	2	19
Postal tax	2	1	44
Postal tax semi-postal	1	Total: 105	
Special delivery	1		
Special handling	1		
Total:	348		

Also of interest is to compare the "top" countries in each of several ways for measuring how active they have been with triangular issues. The total number of issues and the total number of stamps are good measures. The length of time over which they have used triangulars is also important. These measures are presented in the table below.

Top 19 countries in each of three indices

Country	No. of issues	Country	Span of issues	Country	No. of stamps
Liberia	31	Colombia	123 years	Surinam	117
Russia	17	Russia	72	Sharjah	104
Surinam	14	Lithuania	70	Liberia	84
Mongolia	9	Liberia	60	Lithuania	74
Panama	9	Ecuador	57	Panama	70
Tannu Tuva	9	Netherlands	57	Hungary	62
Bolivia	8	Paraguay	55	Mongolia	62
Dominican Republic	8	Salvador, El	53	Monaco	58
Hungary	8	New Zealand	52	Bhutan	52
Latvia	8	Somali Coast	50	Jordan	52
Lithuania	8	Monaco	43	Mali	44
Ecuador	7	Surinam	35	D. Republic	36
Estonia	7	Costa Rica	32	Latvia	34
Monaco	7	Netherlands Antilles	30	Nicaragua	34
Salvador, El	6	Czechoslovakia	28	Russia	32
Bhutan	5	Qatar	28	Paraguay	31
Costa Rica	5	D. Republic	26	Maldive Islands	25
Nicaragua	5	Mongolia	26	Mozambique Company	24
Romania	5	Nicaragua	25	Bolivia	23

Notice that Liberia has had the most issues, the third most number of stamps, and has had triangulars for the fourth longest time period. Compare it with Russia, which is second in number of issues and time span, but way down the list, at 15th, in terms of the number of stamps–many of its issues were a single stamp in the set. Study the table and see what inferences you can draw from it.

Chapter 16

Cinderella Bibliography

The Cinderella items have been extensively researched. This bibliography provides the information needed to find each source used in developing the contents of this handbook. Each reference work has an identification number for use as a "shorthand" notation to a specific book, publication or article. These reference numbers were used in the Cinderella Listing.

This bibliography is in two sections–books and periodicals. Each section is in alphabetical order so you can easily check if a particular reference work has been used in *Triangular Philatelics*.

This bibliography does not include the titles of the many hundreds of books and periodicals I reviewed that had no information on triangulars.

Book references

Reference number	
161	Backman, Anders. *Smaller Channel Islands Catalogue (The)*, 1989.
189	Barata, Paulo Rui. *Selos fiscais de Portugal e Colonias*, 1980.
340	Barefoot, John. *Guernsey and Jersey Revenues*, 1979.
441	Billig, Fritz. *Billig's Philatelic Handbook,* Vol. 1, 19xx.
444	Billig, Fritz. *Billig's Philatelic Handbook*, Vol. 4, 1944.
447	Billig, Fritz. *Billig's Philatelic Handbook*, Vol. 7, 1948.
464	Billig, Fritz. *Billig's Philatelic Handbook*, Vol. 24, 1955.
466	Billig, Fritz. *Billig's Philatelic Handbook*, Vol. 26, 1957.
470	Billig, Fritz. *Billig's Philatelic Handbook*, Vol. 30, 1964.
500	Billig, Fritz. *Billig's Specialized Catalogues*, Vol. 06, 1950
845	Chapier, Georges and Bourdi, A. *Timbres de fantaisie et non officiels: etude historique et descriptive des emissions apocryphes et de fantaisie et des timbres non officiels (Les)* (197?).
865	Chapier, Georges. *Les timbres de Fantaisie avec Supplement*, 197?.
886	Chatfield, Chris, Cinderella Stamp Club (The). *Great Britain Commemorative Labels pre-1950: a catalogue*, 1991.
1005	Covert, Earle L. *Strike, Courier and Local Post of the Elizabethan Era*, 1992.
1255	DuBois, Robert J. *Catalog of Olympic Labels, 1894-1985*, 1986.
1292	Edelis, Tadas. *Catalog of Modern U.S. Local Posts (inc. Canada) Vols. 1 & 2*, 1974.
1326	Eisenhart, Willy. *The World of Donald Evans*, 1980.
1360	Ellington, Jesse T. and Zwisler, Perry F. *Ellington-Zwisler Rocket Mail Catalogue, Vol. 1 (1904-67)*, 1967.
1430	Entwistle, Gordon. *Boy Scout and Girl Guide Stamps of the World*, 1957.
1500	Forbin, A. *Catalogue de Timbres Fiscaux*, 1915.
1570	Fraenkel, H. A. *Postage Stamps From Germany: provincial & local issues 1945-1946*, 1948.
1640	Frajola, Richard C. *Postage Stamps of Siam to 1940: a descriptive catalog (The)*, revised by Richard Ostlie, 1994.
1726	*Galvez Rodriguez, Manuel. Catalogo especializado Galvez de los sellos de Espana, correos y telegrafos, asi como los de sobrecargas patrioticas, sellos de beneficencia, recargo y ayuntamiento de Barcelona, emitidos desde 1850 a 1959*, 1970.
1760	Glasewald, Privatpostmarken Katalog, 1953.
1839	Gottsmich, Severin and Erler, Martin. *CSR Revenue and Railway Stamps*, 1976.
1875	Green, Dick. *Green's Catalog of the Tuberculosis Seals of the World...*, 1979.
1930	Green, Dick. *A Catalog of All Funds Stamps of the USA*, 1930.
1990	Hall, Andrew and Barefoot, John. *Poland Locals*, 1981.

Reference number	
2043	Hellman, E.A. *Eisenbahnmarken Finnlands (Die)*, 1955.
2064	Hellman, Kaj. *Railway Parcel Stamps of Finland (The)*, 1993.
2300	Hornadge, Bill. *Local Stamps of Australia: with a listing of commemorative postalvignettes*, 1982.
2430	Hornadge, Bill. *Cinderella Stamps of Australasia*, 1974.
2566	Irwin, Henry and Mosbaugh, Raymond C. *Mosbaugh's Red Cross Seals of the World Catalog*, 1984.
2700	Jakimovs, J. and Marcilger, V. *The Postal and Monetary History of Latvia 1918-1945*, 1991.
2830	Kanak, Richard C. *Tannu Tuva Catalog*, 1977.
3090	Kessler, F.W. *Rocket Airmail Stamps: a specialized catalogue*, 1935.
3220	Larsen, *Larsen's Sidelines Handbooks*, Vol. 1 No. 3, 1968.
3350	Maksymczuk, *Catalog of foreign private stamps and .... pertaining to Ukraine*, 1962 and 1966 (Russian text).
3480	Martel, Wayne. *Catalogue of 20th Century Local Posts*, (?).
3610	Melville, Fred J. *Phantom Philately*, 1923.
3886	Monde des Philatelistes, Le. *Etude No. 192. Selection philatelique, No. 4.*, 1975.
3930	Morley, Walter. *Catalogue of the Revenue Stamps of South America, a Morley's Philatelic Journal Supplement*, 1904.
4058	*Mosbaugh's U.S. All Funds Seal Catalog*, 1981.
4075	Muller, Frank. *Catalogue des etiquettes aeropostales emises par les Administrations postales, les compagnies de navigation aerienne,etc...*, 1947.
4116	Naudet, Georges. *Vignettes francaises d'aerostation et d'aviation des origines a 1940 (Les)*, (1967?).
4151	Newman, Stanley. *Stamps of Lundy Island: an illustrated priced guide and handbook*, 1989.
4505	Pulinckx, Th. *Luchtpostkataloog*, 1976.
4605	Richet, Roger. *Emissions, surcharges, obliterations et vignettes des Sudetes (1880-1970) (Les)*, 1970.
4672	Rosen, Gerald. *Catalogue of British Postal Strike stamps*, (1971?).
4740	Sanabria's Air Post Catalogue 1963 edition.
4800	Schmidt, Walter E. *Images of the Great War. Volume 1: A fully illustrated catalogue of Delandre's French military vignettes, 1914-1917*, 1984.
5090	Smith, Stephen. Rocket Mail Catalogue, in *Billig's Philatelic Handbook*, Vol. 23, 1956.
5375	Stefanowsky, E.E. *Listing of the Fiscal Stamps of the Soviet Government...* 1962.
5465	Sulser, Heinrich. *Soldatenmarken der Schweiz, 1914/18, 1939/45 (Die)*, 1990.
5560	*Sverige Katalogen 1986-87 Specialkatalog*, Sveriges Filatelist-Forbund, 1986.
5610	*Standard Artist Stamp Catalog*, 4th Edition, 1995, edited by (Dominique) The Bugmaster General.
5660	Wasson, Stanley H. *Catalog of U.S. Philatelic Exhibition Seals*, 1st ed. 1946.
5703	Williams, Leon N. & M. Williams. *Cinderella Stamps*, 1970.
5775	Williams, Marshall M. *A Catalogue of Spanish Local Civil War Madonna Stamps*, 1972.
5990	Zwisler, Perry F. *Ellington-Zwisler Rocket Mail Catalogue*, Vol. 2, 1973.

Periodical references

These references may indicate a span of the periodicals when multiple articles were used. The reference in the listing section provides the specific volume and page numbers for each of the articles.

Reference number	
7030	The American Philatelist, various writings regarding their Black-Blot program and associated steps by other organizations. Vol. 75 (1962)/600, 936; Vol. 76 (1962)/55, 59, 259, 691, 912; Vol. 77 (1964)/477; Vol. 78 (1965)/275, 913, 925; Vol. 81 (1967)/189, 250; Vol. 82 (1968)/177, 273; Vol. 85 (1971)/735, 1,023.
7060	Armstone, John. Ajax Carrier Co. 1971- or 1962?, *The Private Post*, 1980-81.
7090	Odds & Ends, *Atalaya*, Winter 94-95.
7120	Bennett, Lois & Gordon. Swiss Soldier Stamps, *Topical Time*, July 1995.

Reference number	
7150	Bromser, Charles. Elusive Australian Postal Rocket Covers, *The Airpost Journal*, May 1996.
7165	Bromser, Charles and Van Eijck, Bert. Rocket Mail Pioneers, *The Airpost Journal*, a five(?) part series in May 1993, August 1993, (two other issues), September 1994.
7180	Chalfant, Edwin L. Swiss Soldiers' Stamps, *The Cinderella Philatelist*, July 1976.
7240	Chemi, James M. 1964 Spring Meeting Report:..., *The American Philatelist*, July 1964.
7300	Collectors' Forum, *Linn's Stamp News*, Jan. 6, 1992.
7360	Collectors' Forum, *Linn's Stamp News*, July 18 and Aug. 15, 1994.
7375	Collins, Peter. Labels marked Sicily earthquake, *Stamp Collector*, April 2, 1984.
7390	Coyne, Bernard V. The Rattlesnake Island Local Air Post, *The Airpost Journal*, September 1967.
7420	Cullum, J.W. or Rooke, H.F. Modern Bogus Stamps, *The Cinderella Philatelist*, 1961-74.
7480	Herst, Herman Jr. United States Local Delivery, *The Cinderella Philatelist*, January 1967.
7570	Kerrigan, T.M. A Tale of Two Lost Continents, *Scott Stamp Monthly*, January 1983.
7600	Kindler, Jan. Ghosts in the Posts, *Scotts Monthly Stamp Journal*, May 1979.
7615	Kronstein, Dr. Max. The World's Earliest Rocket Start From a High-Altitude Balloon in 1928, *The Airpost Journal*, June 1958.
7630	Lewis, Brenda R. More Philatelic Phantoms, *Scott's Monthly Stamp Journal*, October 1979.
7645	LeShane, A.A. The First International Rocket Mail Flight, *The Airpost Journal*, November 1983.
7660	Martin, Christopher. Would-be Nations of the World, *The Cinderella Philatelist*, April 1970.
7720	McCallum, R. "Kidding" the Post Office - U.S. Style, *The Cinderella Philatelist*, 1961.
7780	Pegg, R.E.F. Modern United States Locals, *The Cinderella Philatelist*, 1961-64.
7840	*Ponwinkle News*, August 1981.
7900	*Poster Stamp Bulletin*, May 1941 through December 1942.
7930	Rapkin, Franceska. Beginners Please, *Stamp Magazine*, March 1981.
7960	Rodestam, Ragnar. Brevmarken vid svenska filatelistevenemang 1911-1970, *Baltespannaren*, Jan. 1984.
8020	Rooke, Harry F. Stepping Beyond the Catalog, *The American Philatelist*, January 1971.
8080	Rooke, Harry F. Stepping Beyond the Catalog, *The American Philatelist*, February 1971.
8140	Rowcroft, Wm. Jr. Rattlesnake Island Local Post, *The Cinderella Philatelist*, January 1967.
8200	*Sanders' Philatelic Journal*, August 1957.
8260	Schultz, William R. Rattlesnake Island: The Only Airmail Local Post, *The Congress Book 1982*.
8320	*Seal News*, 1982-92.
8350	Sente, Marjory J. Shapes & Angles for Stamp Collectors, *Scott's Monthly Stamp Journal*, February 1979, pages 10-13. A general review of the use of different shapes in postage stamps.
8380	Spahich, Eck. Croatia's Exile Issues Convey Aura of Intrigue & Excitement, *Stamp Lover*, February 1995.
8395	*TbBA* (Official Journal of the Tannu Tuva Collectors Society), November 1994.
8410	"The Clubhouse," *The Collector's Club Philatelist*, Vol. 48, #3 (1969).
8440	*The Poster*, Various articles and information items, 1973-96.
8500	*The Poster-Seal Bulletin*, August 1941.
8620	Williams, L.N. & M. Cinderella Corner, *Stamp Magazine*, December 1977.
8680	Williams, L.N. & M. Cinderella Corner, *Stamp Magazine*, June 1978.
8740	Williams, L.N. & M. Cinderella Stamp Corner, *Stamp Magazine*, July 1968.
8860	Williams, L.N. Bahamas: Chub Cay Local Service, *The Cinderella Philatelist*, April 1983.
8920	Winick, Les. The Spotlight is on Lundy Island, *Scott Stamp Monthly*, March 1991.
8945	Wotherspoon, James. British Rocket Flight Experiments Held in 1934, Airpost Journal, August 1948.
8950	Wotherspoon, James. Early Austrian Rocket Flight Experiments, *Airpost Journal*, July 1948.
8980	York, H. The New Zealand Pigeon Post, *The Airpost Journal*, April 1958.

Other references

| 9010 | Kaufmann, Gerhardt (Bill). Pages from his prize-winning rocket mail exhibits. |

General references on stamp collecting

Krause, Barry: *Advanced Stamp Collecting*, 1990. An excellent work for the serious collector. It covers some of the opportunities for a collector beyond just acquiring a collection and knowledge. There are chapters on exhibiting, foreign stamp dealers, stamp societies, stamp museums and libraries, auctions and philatelic writing. *Collecting Stamps for Pleasure & Profit*, 1988. A basic, quick-reading book on stamp collecting. It is worth reading. A good introductory book, especially on collecting tools, stamp condition, stamp periodicals and stamp societies. Unfortunately, "Cinderella" is only an entry in the glossary.

Linn's World Stamp Almanac, published by Amos Press. This hefty volume gives all sorts of perspectives related to stamp collecting. It is worth reading those sections that are of interest to you at a particular time, and then other sections later as your interests change and develop.

Mackay, James. *Stamp Collecting*, 1980. A colorful, well-written, comprehensive overview of stamp collecting in general. Excellent combination of historical flavoring and explanations of major aspects on stamps, what they have been used for, and how they have evolved.

Melville, Fred J. *All About Postage Stamps*, written sometime between 1913-32. This is an old, but well written work, with half of it being an excellent presentation and discussion of the core aspects of philately.

Williams, L. N. & M. *Techniques of Philately*, 1969. One of several excellent books this team of authors produced over the years on philatelic subjects.

Afterword

I hope your use of this handbook leads to as many hours of enjoyable collecting activity as I have found with triangulars. Best of luck searching for and obtaining whatever items will be "real treasures" for you.

I am always looking for more information to add to this handbook to improve its completeness and accuracy. So, if you have suggestions for improvements, please let me know.

For this edition, accuracy was of paramount importance. It is important for the item to actually exist so you do not look for a non-existent item–particularly important when dealing with variations of an item.

This edition does not contain listings of errors, essays, proofs, reprints, minor printing variations, nor minor occurrences of imperf, when perf was the primary separation. In reality, there are items with variations produced in such small quantities they may only be known to specialist collectors of a particular country.

The Cinderella section includes many questions and points regarding getting more complete information. When you can assist with those identified questions, or with information on any new items, please take a few minutes to forward that information to me. A photocopy (Xerox) of the item will be helpful. When the copy is not in color, be sure to identify the colors on the item–similar to the descriptions used herein.

Send all correspondence to:

Chris Green, All Points Philatelics
1609 7th Avenue West
Seattle, WA USA 98119

When you want a reply, be sure to include a legal-size self-addressed envelope stamped with the appropriate USA postage, or international reply coupons for outside the USA.

And finally, I am not a stamp dealer, but I do buy and trade stamps and labels to expand my own collection and to acquire items for use as illustrations in articles and books.